EPOXY
RESIN

EPOXY RESIN

THE COMPLETE GUIDE FOR ARTISTS, BUILDERS, AND MAKERS

Includes 12 step-by-step projects

JESS CROW

Foreword by Mike Holmes

Countryman Press

An Imprint of W. W. Norton & Company
Celebrating a Century of Independent Publishing

Copyright © 2023 by Jess Crow
Foreword © 2023 by Mike Holmes

For information about permission to reproduce selections from this book, write to Permissions, Countryman Press, 500 Fifth Avenue, New York, NY 10110

For information about special discounts for bulk purchases, please contact W. W. Norton Special Sales at specialsales@wwnorton.com or 800-233-4830

Manufacturing by Versa Press
Production manager: Devon Zahn

Countryman Press
www.countrymanpress.com

An imprint of W. W. Norton & Company, Inc.
500 Fifth Avenue, New York, NY 10110
www.wwnorton.com

978-1-68268-780-2

10 9 8 7 6 5 4 3 2 1

To you. I know you didn't think you could do it, and a lot of folks still think you can't. But you got this; you always have.

Minis. Eternity + a day.

CONTENTS

FOREWORD

About four years ago, Jess and I met and instantly connected, sharing our passions for building, creating, and problem-solving. She was launching her business, Crow Creek Designs, and was looking to expand her brand and educate her audience through like-minded people, meaningful connections, and social media. She asked me a ton of questions about building, making things right, and running a business, which I happily answered. She wears her heart on her sleeve, and her drive, love, and compassion for others are captivating. I loved her sunny personality, infectious laugh, and desire to learn anything and everything. I also think she was the first person I'd ever met from Alaska. Since then, we've developed a friendship based on mutual respect and a love of building and learning. We're also both fanatical about a clean workshop and doing things the right way and safely. She's such a talented artist, and I love her work. She has an incredible drive to educate her audience through in-person classes, online tutorials, and now this book. (Congratulations, Jess, on this achievement—you did it!)

I also love educating people and teaching them how to make it right. I know firsthand the enormous power of reaching the masses, whether through my TV shows, online presence, or my books. All are practical tools for educating a larger audience. Knowledge is power, and trying new things helps us grow personally and spiritually, which lies at the core of everything Jess does. At the same time, I always encourage homeowners to do their homework before starting any renovation, big or small. That homework includes understanding the scope of a project, steps involved, best products and practices, necessary tools, and never forgetting about doing it safely. In other words: make it right.

That's precisely what Jess has done in this book. She has shared her knowledge and enthusiasm for designing and creating unique artwork, furniture, and other objects, combining the techniques of epoxy resin with woodworking and painting. The first section provides a short history of the medium, and she has done her own homework, which reveals her in-depth research and experience. She also explores the many facets of working with it, from the fundamentals and effective planning to problem-solving and the finished product. She lays it all out knowledgeably and concisely.

While reading this book, I was thrilled to discover that it's not a craft book. It's an *educational* book. Jess explains the steps required to work with epoxy resin safely, which I love because it can be hazardous if *not* used properly, a point that almost no shows or videos

make. She stresses the importance of fitting a workspace with proper ventilation, such as an exhaust fan or air-exchange system, room temperature and humidity levels, work-surface preparation, mixing utensils, containers and scales, heat gun and torch, and so much more. She also provides simple solutions to common problems that allow you to start small and take the first steps.

Jess's technical understanding comes through in every chapter. She explains the process in a straightforward manner, allowing you to explore the many different uses of epoxy resin easily. She shares her ups and downs, successes and failures, while providing her own best practices, allowing you to benefit from her expertise. Her passion for the medium, how to manipulate it and stretch its possibilities, glows on every page.

The book puts Jess's best practices into action with informative, step-by-step project tutorials at a variety of levels, from beginner to advanced. She guides you every step of the way, with easy-to-follow, detailed descriptions of each one. Her advice is to start small and gradually tackle more significant projects, but if you want to go big, go for it because it just might work out. From learning how to use her line of MakerPoxy to making an Ocean Wave Countertop, you'll build your confidence and skills. Because the projects progress in complexity, following them will help you understand and push the boundaries of the creative process. Learn from your mistakes but be smart about them. I'm not afraid to make mistakes, and neither is she, but this book will help you avoid making some big ones with your own resin work.

Artists, woodworkers, and all creative minds will love this book. It's a well-presented how-to guide and the only one you'll need to work with epoxy resin safely and effectively. Jess Crow's guiding hand will take you on a journey of opportunity and growth. At the end, you'll realize why she has become the "Epoxy Queen."

Mike Holmes

INTRODUCTION

People have been using epoxy resin—a durable, moisture-resistant plastic that forms when resin and hardener mix together at a given ratio—for more than a century, so why hasn't anyone published an all-encompassing book about it before now? The answer is simple. Chemically and physically, epoxy is a dynamic, fluid medium, ever changing into something new.

In 1934, the German government granted chemist Paul Schlack a patent for the "condensation of epoxides and amines," although epoxy resin was in use long before then. In 1943, Schlack and Swiss chemist Pierre Castan laid claim to the discovery of epoxy resins based on bisphenol A, or **BPA**. (Find out more about any terms in bold in the Glossary, page 190.) That year, American chemist Sylvan Greenlee innovated the use of epoxy resin in the dental field. In 1970, brothers Meade and Jan Gougeon built a 35-foot trimaran, *Adagio*, the first boat to use epoxy composite throughout its construction. Word floated quickly through the boating community. The Gougeon brothers became industry leaders, collaborating with Dow Chemical to produce West System Epoxy. Their reputation for excellence and innovation also drew them beyond the marine market. In 1979, NASA researchers hired the Gougeons' company to build experimental blades for wind turbines. Since those early days of discovery, epoxy resins have gone into myriad industrial applications, most familiarly on boats and in heavy machinery. Surfboards, skateboards, and flooring all use epoxy for laminating and coating, as do other perhaps surprising household products: textiles, paper, paint cans, and other metal items prone

to rusting. A thin coat of epoxy can help protect and extend the life of all those items and many more. Strong, pliable, and beautiful, it can mimic the look of countless man-made and natural materials.

Early epoxy resins sometimes looked yellowish, but the epoxy itself wasn't yellow. That effect resulted from the hardener, which also could become brittle when cured. Early work with the medium required precise-to-the-gram measurements and—no joke—a hazmat suit. Some epoxies still include those requirements, so it's vital to know exactly which products have them. Thankfully manufacturers have designed more user-friendly formulas, such as MakerPoxy, with both people and the environment in mind. Old and new formulas still sit side by side on store shelves, though, because each has a place in the modern workspace. For example, if you're building a boat, a **high-performance epoxy** always will work better than a **1:1 formula**. Why? High-performance

epoxy better suits a technique called **glassing** as well as **wet** and **hand layups**.

In early 2018, one of my clients, a tattoo artist, wanted a queen bed. If you ever have met any tattoo artists, you know how particular they can be about their likes and dislikes. She had two extremely specific requests for her build: it needed a whale, and it needed a galaxy. No pressure! That bed nudged me into epoxy resin (figuratively of course). The galaxy, painted *on* a 5½-foot-long wooden whale, needed visual depth without adding tons of volume, which epoxy resin could achieve and did. "This bed is going to make me go viral!" I told her. It didn't, but, hey, all good things in time. With that build, I started exploring epoxy resin more deliberately. Everything about it was a learning process, and nothing went according to plan.

Epoxy has a mind of its own and does whatever it wants to do, regardless of what you want. My trial-and-error experiences led to surprising discoveries, epic pivots, and, in the end, the best

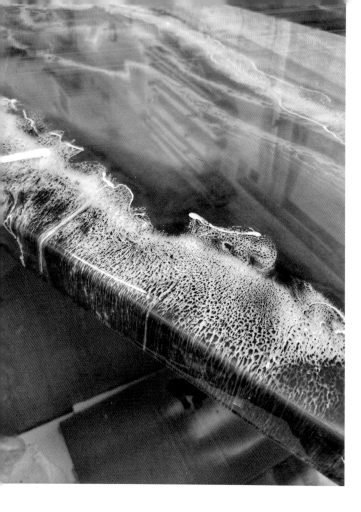

practices contained in this book. Those experiences taught me how to manipulate epoxy and stretch its possibilities beyond my existing point of reference and even imagination. Questions exploded in my brain—sometimes through tears—as I stood in front of failed projects. *How much color can I add before the epoxy* **seizes**? *How long can I wait before doing a pour? Um, is it supposed to be* smoking *like that?*

My next big build, which started at the end of 2018, did go viral: the original Ocean Wave Countertop that has become a staple in the epoxy and woodworking world. Bernie's Bungalow, a local restaurant, wanted a new counter for their sushi station. They had seen artwork online with hand-painted waves coated in epoxy and wanted to know whether I could do that on a large scale. Sure, why not?

Flash forward two years, and I have my own

line of epoxy: MakerPoxy by Jess Crow in partnership with TotalBoat. This epoxy bridges the gap between products often called building epoxies and art epoxies. Building epoxies have the necessary strength for use on furniture, boats, and other major structures. But they can yellow early and have a short **pot life** and pour depth. (More on both topics later.) Art epoxies, on the other hand, have a reputation for clarity and extended pot life, but they don't have enough strength to withstand heavy use on countertops or tables. Thanks to its adaptability, clarity, durability, ease of use, and safety, Maker-Poxy by Jess Crow has become one of the most known and respected epoxies on the market.

Online tutorials and videos of epoxy resin may have captivated you, yet when you dive in to the mechanics of the medium, it suddenly can seem too expensive and daunting. Any confidence you might have had flies out the window. But the projects in part four of this book (page 83) will encourage you to start with something simple to build your confidence and skills. Before you do that, however, read through the whole book and *all* the projects before selecting one. You don't need to start small and then tackle bigger projects—I didn't. But starting small will save you money up front and give you the self-assurance to move forward.

As you're learning how to use epoxy resin in your creative projects, remain resolutely open-minded about the results. Thousands of students have taken my classes in person and hundreds of thousands more online. Those who achieve the best results don't necessarily have the most experience or skills, but they all have open minds. Regardless of your level of experience, keeping your mind open to how a project *might* work out, rather than focusing rigidly on how it *must* work out, will lead you down the best path to success. In addition to helping you work safely, this book offers you the advantage of learning from all my mistakes and failures over the years so that you don't have to repeat them. In these pages, you'll find answers to all the questions I asked myself while watching projects go sideways in my shop, plus helpful responses to my many students' questions and concerns.

Epoxy resin is an exacting, sometimes finicky medium, so it's essential to fully understand its ebb and flow. You may ask, "Why am I seeing tons of bubbles in the work I did yesterday?" or "Why did it start smoking when I added this acrylic paint, but another brand worked fine?" Maybe you've sought answers to those questions by watching tutorials online, stalking social media sites, or reading other books about resin and woodworking. If you still have questions, you've come to the right place. Sure, you can glean the bare-bones basics from videos or social media, but you deserve a lot more than just the bare minimum. This book provides all the information you need but won't find for free online—plus a dozen guided projects with ideas for even more variations. It divulges all the trade secrets you need to know for a successful pour every time.

The 12 projects in part four introduce you slowly and with intent to the art of working with epoxy resin. Instead of leaping into a huge, expensive project, you'll get your properly protected hands dirty with more manageable projects that light a fire in you to tackle larger builds. My approach in each project derives, in part, from Jodi Picoult's *The Book of Two Ways*. Her novel has nothing to do with epoxy, but its title and premise inspired me to present the projects in this book in two ways: using items readily available at local stores

or making them yourself. If the latter option seems at all daunting, rest assured that the book contains mostly projects that anyone can make on a TV tray.

It's also important to understand that you really do have a million and one ways to do any given task at any given time in any given place. That's part of what makes epoxy's overlap with the art, builder, and maker communities so much fun. Follow this book like a favorite hiking trail, but don't be afraid to veer (safely) onto your own path.

"Build more than furniture" has served as my mantra for a long time. Woodworking, epoxy work, and art don't have to result in tables, dressers, or statement pieces. "Build more than furniture" means build more confidence, build more skills, build more memories.

The epoxybilities are endless.

PART ONE

THE FUNDAMENTALS

1

ESSENTIAL TERMS AND SAFETY

Failure Spelled Backward Is Learning

One of the biggest mistakes that you can make when working with epoxy—and it happens in my own work and in my classes all the time—is thinking that you have total control over this medium. You can control only your approach and response to epoxy. It has a mind of its own and does what *it* wants to do.

As you read through this book, you'll learn the difference between controlling epoxy and manipulating it. You *control* epoxy when you choose the right resin for a project, plan the weight of a piece—a frequently overlooked component of a build—and how to finish it, prepare your workstation properly, and use **personal protective equipment (PPE)** correctly. You *manipulate* epoxy when you introduce heat with a **heat gun** or, conversely, when you don't. You'll discover a lot more about this technique throughout the book, but it boils down to this: When you use a heat gun, you not only eliminate bubbles, but you also cause the epoxy to expand and contract. We're not ready yet to geek out on how the weights of different chemicals, **pigments**, and dyes affect how they settle into the epoxy, so here's the short version. When you heat epoxy and introduce multiple additives, each with a different weight, the heat causes the epoxy to expand, and heavier additives settle to the lower range of the epoxy, much the way sediment or particulate settles at the bottom of a glass. When you remove the heat, the epoxy will contract. If a lighter-weight pigment is sitting in the middle, it will rise to the top, creating magnificent veins of color, whereas, again, a heavier pigment will sink to the bottom. This chemistry creates fascinating results that look like fissures. By manipulating epoxy with a heat gun, you can achieve almost any effect you want.

When you start your epoxy journey, learn to master manipulation. Keep a workbook or make detailed notes in your phone as you brainstorm new projects. If you do, you'll notice patterns of how added powders, pigments, inks, and other additives settle in the epoxy. It's a lot of fun to experiment in a controlled environment but not under pressure. Many of my own pours have gone sideways because I didn't fully understand the chemistry of a given project. Allow me to tell you about the Black Burn (circa January 2019).

A client wanted something to remind her of the Hawaiian Islands. In my quest to capture the effect of hardened lava flows in a group of tables, I experimented with embedding colored epoxy in burned wood. But *thousands* of micro-bubbles rose from every part of the wood. The reason was simple. As a liquid, epoxy will find every nook and cranny of an object into which you pour it. It's like when a ship sinks and air pockets form in sealed rooms. Air always finds its way to the top, and the top in this case was all the lovely wood purchased and prepped for the project. Not only did the air pockets make it hard to keep the color inside the burned sections of wood, but creating the look of lava shiny but matte, hard but pillowy-looking—also proved exceptionally challenging.

Heading back to the drawing board, I burned more wood to capture the look of lava, as intended. Then I used a different oil-based sealant to seal the wood before working on it with colored epoxy. My main mistake? I went BIG without testing it first. I tried to control the epoxy, and I didn't take the time to learn how to *manipulate the epoxy*. That experiment took almost two weeks of trial and mostly error before yielding a solution. In the meantime, I had to explain to my client why her island tables were going to take another two weeks. Not good. The best way to avoid this type of error is to experiment with different woods, wood sealants, pigments, and finishes on a small scale *before* tackling the full project. Now you know.

FORMULAS

Even with newer formulas, epoxy resins can present serious hazards to your health when used improperly. Thankfully, they're a far cry from the industrial epoxies used in the 1930s and '40s—and even just 20 years ago. Commercial-grade applications use a handful of job-specific epoxies, but we're going to focus primarily on the epoxies you most likely will use in your workspace or home:

- UV resin (often mistakenly called "UV epoxy")
- **casting epoxy** or polyurethane epoxies
- thick-set or deep-pour epoxy
- art or coating epoxy
- multipurpose epoxy
- penetrating or sealing epoxy

Other types of epoxies you may encounter include:

- polyester
- fairing

These main groups include a variety of subclasses. For instance, when using a TotalBoat **High-Performance Epoxy**, you can choose among slow, medium, and fast hardeners, meaning the speed at which epoxy will cure. A fast hardener works best in a cool, dry environment when you want a fast cure. In a warm environment and with a longer working time, a medium hardener works best. If you want the longest time possible to experiment, choose a slow hardener. Manufacturers make hardeners (called "**part B**") that they designate as "tropical" because they work best in hot, humid environments. In those settings, the hardener works as slowly as possible to account for the warmth and water content of the ambient air, giving you more time to lay it out. With another kind, you might not make it from mixing cup to project surface!

"Why Is It Yellow?"

If, at some point, you wonder, *Why does this epoxy look like . . . urine?*, have a good laugh and understand that you're looking at the hardener, not the epoxy. Manufacturers formulate some hardeners to have a yellow or amber color. Other hardeners yellow quickly, within one or two weeks, just sitting on the shelf. Eventually all consumer epoxy will yellow without a UV protection coat added as part of yearly maintenance. MakerPoxy contains UV inhibitors, but that only buys you time. It won't eliminate yellowing indefinitely.

Also note that UV resins aren't the same as products labeled "UV stable" or "UV inhibitors added." UV resin cures specifically under a UV light, which can come from a UV flashlight or, more commonly, a **UV light bar**, like the ones that nail salons use (page 203). Light bars offer a broader field of UV light than a flashlight and can cure UV epoxy quickly and evenly.

No product currently on the market is 100 percent UV stable. Epoxies, such as MakerPoxy, contain UV inhibitors to reduce the damage caused by UV exposure, but you still need to apply a UV protection **topcoat** if you plan on keeping your project outside or in an area that receives frequent direct sunlight. For those situations, you want a product such as Halcyon varnish (page 73).

Let's look at a few more key phrases.

TERMS

Pot life means the amount of time that the epoxy will remain liquid, at the temperature recommended by the manufacturer, once the resin and the hardener make contact or, in the case of UV resin, when UV light hits it.

Ratios refer to the amount of epoxy, or **part A**, mixed with hardener, or part B. A 1:1 ratio contains equal amounts of epoxy and hardener. A 3:1 ratio contains three parts A (epoxy) to one part B (hardener). In the supplies section (page 32), you'll learn how to measure epoxy and hardener properly, and in the chapter planning chapter (page 35) you'll learn which type of epoxy to use for different projects. Different brands recommend different ways of doing things, meaning that something simple to understand about one brand may seem a lot harder to grasp about another. Thankfully these terms and ratios hold across all brands and learning platforms.

ESSENTIAL SAFETY

Every single one of these safety directives is nonnegotiable. Consider yourself warned!

- Always keep pets and small children away from uncured epoxy resin.
- Always work in a well-ventilated area and wear a respirator rated for chemical use.
- Always wear safety goggles and have an eyewash kit and/or station ready to use.
- Always be prepared to remove epoxy resin from your skin with soap and water.
- Always wear gloves when handling any epoxy resin product.
- Never leave epoxy resin unattended in an area containing combustible items.

Now let's take a deeper dive in to how to responsibly protect yourself, others, and the environment while working with epoxy.

2

PROPER PROTECTION

Don't Eat Epoxy in Bed

From an environmental and health standpoint, epoxy has a bad rap—and rightfully so. Just a few clicks on the Internet will lead you to groups devoted to how lousy epoxy is for the world at large and your health in particular. This chapter won't address every single concern about epoxy resin, but it will give you the knowledge you need to make informed decisions about the products you use in order to lessen their impact on the environment and protect the health of the people and animals around you as well as your own.

DATA SHEETS

Are you old enough to remember paper road maps? If not, how about the 10-page instruction pamphlet to assemble your first flat-pack shoe rack or bookshelf? Everybody loves a shortcut, famously called the longest distance between two points by economist Charles Issawi. We all want to skip ahead, cut to the chase, or consult a favorite online discussion group whenever we can. But with epoxy, you always need to read all the instructions. Here's why.

Epoxy comes in many formulas, and every formula has a unique smell, mix time, **pot life**, additive limit, **cure time**, and sanding constraint. Manufacturers provide **data sheets** and product information on the label, which will help you eliminate 90 percent of the problems you could encounter. For example, you need to know whether the manufacturer recommends or *requires* using a mask or respirator. Some epoxies can't pour at more than $\frac{1}{8}$ inch deep at one time, while others must pour at least 3 inches deep. The many differences between brands can lead to confusion. For instance, can you use garage floor epoxy on a kitchen counter?

You'll learn more about the different kinds of epoxy in the effective planning chapter (page 35). If you're making a 2-inch-deep table (page 72), you want a thick-set or deep-pour epoxy. If you're pouring a small **mold** or creating wall art (page 72), you want a dual-use,

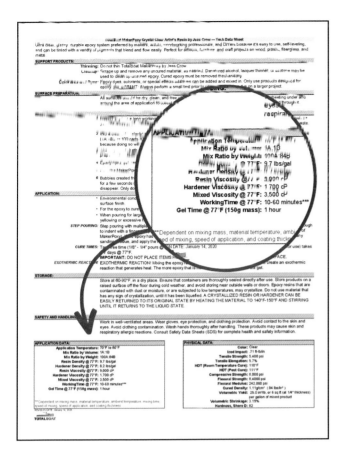

crossover epoxy such as MakerPoxy, an art epoxy, or a tabletop formula with a thicker viscosity. A material safety data sheet (**MSDS**) spells out how long you have to pour, how deep you can pour, and how long the epoxy needs to cure fully. These critical pieces of information allow you to plan ahead properly and not waste epoxy or endure unnecessary exposure to it.

SMALL ANIMALS AND CHILDREN

Birds, cats, and small dogs have a particular susceptibility to airborne chemicals. Folks buy epoxy from unscrupulous companies that don't provide data sheets all the time, and many of those purchasers experience heartache when their small animals subsequently die from long-term exposure to epoxy fumes. *Don't use any epoxy that doesn't come with a clear data sheet.* Never. I don't care if it's cheaper. Your health and the well-

being of children and pets are worth far more than saving a few dollars on a dodgy product.

Using epoxy around or with children under age 12 or 13 remains controversial. On the one hand, you may want to encourage their creativity, but on the other, you certainly don't want to expose them to hazardous chemicals. To proceed responsibly, you *must* read data sheets completely, work in a well-ventilated area, and fit the children with **PPE** designed for their smaller bodies. An adult respirator won't fit a small child correctly. When working with any epoxy and kiddos, you need smaller gloves and goggles, too. Another great way to encourage kids' creativity while using epoxy safely is to modify your workstation. Use a small step stool at the proper height to prevent them from getting too close to a project.

SMELLS AND FUMES

The medical term for having a heightened sense of smell is hyperosmia. If you can smell perfume, cologne, or other scents from about 80 feet (25 meters) away, you likely will have a sensitivity to all epoxy smells. Manufacturers have created some newer epoxies without **BPA**, including MakerPoxy, for use indoors with ventilation, but some people still find the smell off-putting.

Epoxy requires a reaction —**part A** + **part B**— to create the finished product. To avoid becoming part of that **chemical reaction**, you need to wear a respirator. The market offers multiple types, from standard respirators that require only periodic cartridge changes to fully self-enclosed respirators with filtered air packs. Whichever you choose, verify that the manufacturer rates the respirator for working with **volatile organic compounds (VOCs)**. If you work in a small shop or garage, invest in a **powered air-purifying respirator (PAPR)**. They can cost you some coin, but they're worth the money in the long run because they'll save you money on disposable filter packs. On the other hand, PAPRs, fully enclosed face respirators, can feel overwhelming for anyone with claustrophobia.

PPE

Fabric aprons are useless. Go for leather or waxed canvas aprons made from thick, wax-treated cotton duck (also called duck cloth), which helps repel epoxy and acts as a significant barrier between your clothing and the apron. If you do use a fabric apron, tape a piece of plastic—triple-layered plastic wrap or, better yet, heavy-duty painter's plastic sheeting—across your midsection to keep epoxy from seeping into the apron, into your clothing, and onto your skin.

If you're working anywhere near heavy machinery, wear steel-toed footwear or newer, lighter styles made with carbon fiber. If you're working only with epoxy, wear shoes made from tightly woven materials or, better still, plastic shoes with no holes. These kinds of footwear will prevent epoxy drips from seeping through the shoes, through your socks, and onto your feet, and they're easy to clean. My workshop shoes have a carbon fiber toe and a closed-knit top that allows my feet to breathe without allowing epoxy drips to penetrate the weave.

Safety glasses can protect your eyes only so much from a splash or spill. Invest in goggles. They wrap around your face and glasses, if you wear them, to protect your eyes from any mishaps from any angle. Highly viscous thick-sets and deep-pours easily can splash in your face when you pour them. Have an eye-flush kit on hand and set up an eyewash station wherever you plan on working. *If epoxy gets in your eyes, seek medical help immediately.*

EPOXY MOUTH

If you snickered at the subtitle for this chapter, you need to know that I made that statement in all seriousness. When I warn my students not to eat epoxy, they all laugh and ask, "Who would do that?" All my students start the class aghast at the prospect but confident that it won't happen to them. But of the hundreds of classes I've taught, in only a handful did people *not* end up with epoxy in or nearly in their mouth. It can happen so easily.

It happens when you're concentrating on a pour and you reflexively use a gloved hand—covered in epoxy, of course—to remove a stray hair from your mouth. It happens, as you're leaning over a project, when your glasses start sliding down your nose and, without thinking, you push them back up with your epoxy-covered glove, which accidentally touches your mouth. My personal favorite happens when you stand back to admire your project in all its glory. Looking at your gloved hands and realizing how much epoxy you have on them, you try to remove your gloves with your *teeth*. (Don't do that.)

While working with epoxy, awareness of all parts of your body at all times ensures both safety and success. Overriding natural instincts—touching your face, hair, glasses, and clothing—takes practice but remains necessary. Here are some more crucial instructions:

- Don't eat epoxy. Yes, I'm saying it again. It doesn't matter whether it has cured or not. Don't do it.
- Don't pour epoxy down the drain.
- Don't dispose of any epoxy, epoxy-covered items, or epoxy-related waste in the trash. Take it to the hazardous waste area at your local dump.
- Follow all essential safety guidelines (page 22).

FOOD SAFETY

Countless social media groups spend hours every day arguing about this topic, calling technical assistance lines to express their concerns, receiving advice, and finding ways to use epoxy safely. So is epoxy resin **safe for contact with food?**

Yes—and no.

That answer's about as clear as a bucket of smoking, ruined resin tinted brown, huh? Let me explain. In a liquid state and uncured, epoxy and products such as UV resin are hazardous chemicals and *not* safe for contact with food or on surfaces that food may contact. Cured epoxy filled with inedible objects—glitter, spray paint, spent shell casings, anything else you want to include or embed—also is *not* safe for contacting food. If you normally wouldn't put something in your mouth, don't allow food to contact the epoxy project containing the item, no matter what it is. You also don't want to use it for any items, such as cups or bowls, that could have direct mouth contact. Artists, builders, chemists, makers, manufacturers, and PhDs all confirm that no consumer epoxy can go in the microwave, oven, or any other vessel used to heat food. Heating cured epoxy can result in the release of hazardous fumes and toxic chemicals into the food being heated.

But.

When inert, meaning fully cured, epoxy and UV resin—when stated explicitly by the manufacturer's **MSDS** and, if tints or pigments have been added, with a properly applied **flood coat** or **topcoat**—are typically safe for contact with food on an *occasional* basis. In Chapter 8: Sanding and Finishing (page 62), you'll learn how to make your projects safer around food, and the Resources section (page 202) can help you make additional informed decisions about your work.

CLEAN UP

It doesn't matter whether you're using 1 teaspoon of epoxy or 50 gallons. Don't dispose of epoxy by pouring it down the drain or throwing it in the trash. It's vital to find the right balance between successfully executing epoxy projects and interacting responsibly with the environment. Every local dump has a hazardous waste area. Collect empty containers, used gloves, and anything else that has come into contact with the epoxy and take it to your local hazardous waste disposal site for them to handle. You'll have to pay for that service, but it's the right thing to do and well worth the minimal cost.

Using leftover epoxy, rather than dumping it, whether cured or uncured, also reduces your impact on the environment. If you have leftover epoxy, use it for another project. Here's another way that keeping a workbook or notes with an "ideas for future projects" section can pay off. Having a selection of clean silicone molds on hand makes it easy to pour in any leftover epoxy. The molds can make small gifts—such as coasters, wall hangers, and other decorations—or smaller constituent pieces for mosaics, sun catchers, bowl turning, and much more. Also consider using your leftovers for tests or experimentation.

If epoxy touches your skin, use soap or baking soda and vinegar—in that order—to clean it. Some companies make special epoxy resin cleaners, but double-check that they're safe for use on skin. Manufacturers design some epoxy cleaners for use only on nonporous surfaces, and your skin is very porous. If you spill epoxy on a cleanable surface, the best way to prevent it from becoming a problem is to wipe it immediately with a wet wipe. Next, use denatured alcohol to remove any remaining residue. Sometimes you can do this immediately, mid-pour. But if you're using epoxy with a 10-minute pot life, you can't stop in the middle of the pour, so you may need to use some extra elbow grease to clean it up when you're done.

3

PREPARATION AND SUPPLIES

Rain Boots for Epoxy Puddles

In this chapter, you'll learn how to prep properly for builds and pours. Preparing your workspace and choosing the right tools before you start working will ensure good safety and successful projects. Planning pays off. With proper preparation, reducing consumables will help save you money, and having a ready supply of everything you need for building and pouring will save you from wasting time, scrambling in a panic to find gloves, mixing sticks, or colorant when your epoxy has reached a critical state. More often than not, you'll spend more on consumables—such as mixing sticks and gloves for before, during, and after a pour—than the epoxy itself. In addition to **PPE**, you'll need mixing containers—large or small, depending on the project—a **heat gun**, and other key supplies. You also may need to make some modifications to them to create a safe, usable workspace.

VENTILATION

When setting up a workspace properly, you must ventilate both the working area and the project itself. "My *project* needs ventilation?" you might ask. Yep, the project itself. Some **large pours** and even small ones with a lot of volume need ventilation to avoid overheating. Have you ever left your phone on a warm surface and, when you picked it back up, it felt scalding hot? Its battery heat and the surface heat worked hand in hand to accelerate overheating. The same phenomenon can happen with an epoxy project. If you're working outdoors, ventilation poses less of an issue than, say, in an unventilated 5-by-5-foot room with no windows. In the latter situation, you'd need to install a vent fan or **air-exchange system** to avoid exposure to fumes and to prevent them from migrating into other unwanted locations. If you're working in a room with a window, installing an air-exchange fan, like the one below, and using a respirator will reduce your exposure and everyone else's to potentially harmful fumes.

If you're working with epoxy in a shop, install an **air cleaner** above the area where you plan to work. It will pull fumes from the shop. Wearing proper PPE in this setting also will help ensure a safe work environment that you can use long term.

WORKSPACE TEMPERATURE

People frequently overlook this important detail. If you want to achieve a smooth, mirror-like finish on your epoxy work, you need to use a **self-leveling formula**, such as MakerPoxy, gently allowing it to reach and complete its peak **exothermic reaction** (more on this later). If your workspace runs too hot or too cold, the **ambient temperature** will affect the epoxy and hardener in their containers as well as the final results. You can store everything comfortably between 60°F and 80°F, but experience has taught me that epoxy stores and works best at 72°F to 75°F.

When prepping a pour in an unstable environment, you need to stabilize the temperature, even just in the short term. Using a small portable heater or air-conditioning unit to hit the 72°F to 75°F sweet spot will allow your pour to stay at the correct temperature while it cures. To manage temperature while working with epoxy is one of the top three ways to succeed with this sometimes tricky medium. (The other two are choosing the right epoxy for the right project and measuring and mixing correctly.) When using any portable heating system, *never* leave it unattended. Doing so can result in a fire that destroys property and lives.

Humidity also affects **pot life** and **cure times**. A location with high heat and humidity will reduce pot life by around 25 percent, depending on the type of epoxy. If you live in a high-humidity area, invest in a workshop

dehumidifier to reduce the water content of the air, which will allow your epoxy to cure at the right speed. Do a timed experiment with the product you plan on using to test the pot life and cure time of your specific pour location. Mix a small batch of epoxy in a mixing cup and monitor the time it takes to become hot and then to gel. If the result varies from the pot life specified on the **data sheet**, the temperature and moisture of the ambient air likely are playing a role.

SURFACE PREPARATION

Overlooking surface coverings can cost you big-time. Some makers use plastic sheeting or thick paper as a disposable barrier to protect a table or workstation from inevitable overspill. To eliminate this cost completely, invest in sheets of highly durable plastic, such as ultra-high molecular weight (**UHMW**) or high-density polyethylene (**HDPE**). Either make a workstation protector from one of those materials or purchase smaller sheets and move them from one workstation to another. Cured epoxy doesn't stick to UHMW or HDPE, and you can use both to make your own molds.

If, because of budgetary constraints, you need to use plastic to cover your workstation, a few great options have a longer life than plastic sheets. Vinyl tablecloths, available at discount, party supply, and thrift stores, offer a great alternative to single-use plastics. Ugly tablecloths usually cost less, too! If plastic sheeting remains your only option, select the thickest one you can find, meaning the product with the highest **mil** thickness. A 6-mil sheet supplies extra-heavy-duty protection, and you can use it multiple times.

MIXING UTENSILS

The rise of silicone baking tools has become a huge boon for the world of epoxy resin because epoxy doesn't stick to silicone, either. This lucky phenomenon makes the baking supplies aisle of your local supermarket or home store a paradise for reusable mats, molds, cups, and spatulas. These items, which you can use over and over, reduce a lot of waste and keep costs down. After you mix your epoxy with a silicone stir stick, allow the epoxy to cure on it. Then simply bend the stick or slap it against a stable surface, and the bond between the epoxy and the stick will break so you can use the stick again. If any epoxy remains stuck, use denatured alcohol to remove it. Use denatured alcohol to clean all your silicone utensils and containers after use.

If you can't find silicone utensils or if you use popsicle sticks instead, this cost-effective tip will maximize using them. Buy a bulk box of tongue depressors. Break each one in half widthwise and then in half lengthwise to create four smaller sticks. Each quarter can collect **mica powder** and mix small amounts of epoxy perfectly.

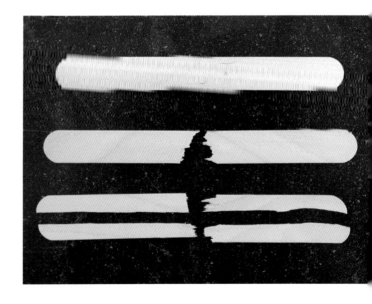

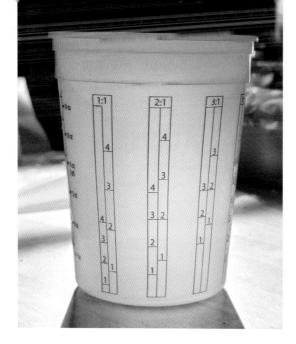

CONTAINERS, CUPS, AND SCALES

Always note whether the epoxy you're using requires measurement by weight or volume. Each manufacturer uses its own method. It would be nice if we had one easy-to-understand methodology for all of them, but then epoxy work wouldn't be so much fun, would it?

If you need to mix by weight, cover your scale with plastic wrap from the grocery store to protect it from spills or drips. After placing your cup on the weighing pad, always hit the zero or tare button, depending on the scale. Measure the appropriate amounts of **part A** and **part B** into the cup and mix accordingly.

For mixing epoxy, look for heavy plastic containers, particularly paint-mixing cups, in the painting section of any home store. The containers usually feature measurements on the outside as well as a **ratio** calculator alongside the standard ounce and mL markings. These ratio calculations helpfully indicate the proper volumes of epoxy and hardener. The image at the top illustrates how they work. The upper numbers indicate whether the measurement will hit a 1:1, 2:1, or 3:1 ratio and so on. In the measuring, mixing,

coloring, and pouring chapter (page 46), you'll learn in depth how to use this style of cup. You can reuse these heavy-duty cups, too. Let the epoxy cure fully inside them while leaving in the tongue depressor you used for mixing or adding one along the inside wall of the container. Once the epoxy has cured, roll the container between your hands or on a stable surface to loosen the bond. Then pull on the tongue depressor, using it as a lever to extract the cured epoxy. Remove any remaining epoxy that hasn't cured in the container with denatured alcohol.

HEAT GUN AND TORCH

Ah, the eternal debate. If you've watched people working with epoxy resin on social media, you'll see which tool they favor. Everyone has a favorite, but your toolkit has room for both.

A **torch** works fantastically well for thick-set pours and quick flashes of heat over a small silicone mold to remove bubbles. But a torch can't blend colors or create the effect of waves. That's a job for a heat gun, which can pop bubbles and blend colors. But using a heat gun to pop bubbles in a small mold could blow some of the epoxy from the mold by accident. A small cooking torch or hardware store butane torch works perfectly for almost all pours. Heat guns can prove a bit trickier. Some heat guns have a lot of air but not a lot of heat. Others have a lot of heat but little air. Problems arise when these components fall out of balance.

When choosing a heat gun, find one that has variable settings, either low and high or medium and high. If you want a glassy finish for your project, you need to reduce the amount of heat you introduce at any time so you don't **toast** the epoxy. Also look at the trigger mechanism. You're a magical unicorn, but you still will

end up with epoxy on your tooling. If you notice right away, you might have time to clean it off. If you don't notice until later, it can prove very challenging to remove the cured epoxy. I went through a few heat guns before settling on the Wagner FURNO 300 (page 203). I never deviate from using it. The Wagner FURNO 300 is the most stable, steadfast heat gun I've used. Even after three years and hundreds of sticky-gloved pours, I'm still using the same one. The switch on this model allows you to use a small mallet or the edge of a table to release any epoxy that inevitably will get on the handle.

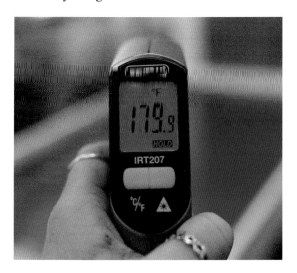

EPOXY TEMPERATURE

The temperature of packaged epoxy and hardener matters just as much as the temperature of the ambient air. You may have heard about using a water bath to warm cold epoxy. In my opinion, that's a terrible idea that can end up costing you a lot of money.

Water is the nemesis of epoxy, preventing it from mixing or curing properly. If you use it to warm your epoxy, you risk water dripping from one of the containers when you remove it from the water bath. Even if you wipe off all the drips, you might not have wiped off *all* the drips. One pesky little drop of water falling into the exact amount of part A mixed perfectly with the precise measure of part B will make you face the choice of tossing the entire mint or putting a portion of uncured epoxy.

How to avoid that panic-inducing nightmare? Use a heating pad or electric blanket. Buy one from your local thrift, dollar, or big-box store. It removes the risk of water fouling your mixture, and lots of models allow you to set the exact temperature and even a timer to warm your epoxy and hardener before you start to work in your workspace.

4

EFFECTIVE PLANNING

The Best-Laid Schemes

Epoxy comes in formulations ranging from 1:1 all the way to 25:1, but what do those **ratios** mean? An epoxy project doesn't end once you've poured the liquid and have a bubble-free, dust-free finish. Unless you've planned your project thoroughly, any number of details can catch you off guard and ruin the result you want.

Here's a familiar scenario. After laboring for more than three weeks, you complete the best table you've ever done. Now it's time to attach the legs. Except you realize, your stomach dropping, that you can't attach the legs where they should go. Why? For structural integrity, their attach points lie smack in the middle of your beautiful, colorful epoxy pour. To attach the legs, you need to drill into the epoxy, and you're going to see every one of those bolts. Disasters like that are why you need to plan every step of your project in advance: from first drop of epoxy to placement of last bolt. You don't often see or hear about important, demystifying steps like these on social media. This chapter arms you with all the planning tools you'll need to execute a successful pour and finished project.

TYPES OF EPOXY

Deciding which epoxy to use for a project can prove hard even for experienced folks because the market offers so many types that you can use most of the time. Discovering which epoxy *not* to use can be a real buzzkill for any maker, builder, or artist, however. The wrong choice of epoxy or improper preparations can leave your tools epoxied to the floor or, worse yet, you *and* your pants epoxied to the floor, as happened to my friend Trent, fraught with fatigue and stress, while building a canoe (*Little and Often* by Trent Preszler). If that has happened to you, know that you're not alone.

Too many people think *Eh, this should be OK*, only to discover all too dramatically that their choice was definitely not OK at all. Proper preparation, as discussed in the previous chapter, will carry you a lot of the way but not to the finish line—not just yet. First, you need to choose the right epoxy for the project you have in mind. Knowing how to make the right choice will enable the successful execution of any project you undertake, making it one of the most important aspects of this book.

In the essential terms and safety chapter, you learned about the most common types of epoxy resin on the consumer market. Of those, only a few will work for artwork, a river-style table, or coating a counter or tabletop. The dearth of information about which epoxies best suit specific projects can leave you feeling confused and angry, particularly if the project you tried to re-create from YouTube devolved into a smoking pile of rubbish. When shopping, you'll notice that some products feature more information than others. That's because some epoxies have more versatility than others.

The following survey of epoxy types indicates what works best for which kind of project. Each entry gives average or typical **pot life** ranges. Each product and brand has its own specific details, so *always* default to the information on the label. The same rule holds true of the given ratio. I provide the normal proportions, but norms aren't definitive. Understanding them thoroughly, however, will help you learn new ways to expand the boundaries of your work.

Art Epoxy

Some of the most versatile products on the market, art epoxies were my favorites until crossover epoxies came along. They have some of the longest pot lives and residual working times on the market, making them incredibly easy to use. They give you a long time to manipulate the epoxy to get the effects you want. They contain little to no **VOCs** and no **BPA**. Some user-friendly art epoxies work extremely well for small crafting projects. Typically they have longer pot lives and cure extremely clear. The downside: You can use them only to coat artwork because they don't have the requisite strength for use on furniture or other items that need to withstand heavy use. Art epoxy works best when showcasing the beautiful artwork beneath it.

BRANDS: MakerPoxy by TotalBoat and Jess Crow, Art Resin, UVPoxy by EcoPoxy
POT LIFE: 60–90 minutes
RATIO: 1:1

Coating Epoxy

As the name indicates, coating epoxy is a great product to use for coating projects, both artwork and furniture. Some formulas are self-leveling, which does a lot of the work to achieve a professional finish when the epoxy has cured. Often containing no BPA and low or no VOCs, they are extremely durable, and with an easy to use 1:1 formula, they are the most commonly used types for coating furniture or counters. Some formulas have a 20-minute pot life, such as TableTop, whereas crossover epoxies (next section) have a 60- to 90-minute pot life. Read the instructions.

> **BRANDS:** MakerPoxy by TotalBoat and Jess Crow, Table Top by TotalBoat, MirrorCoat by System Three
>
> **POT LIFE:** 20–90 minutes
>
> **RATIO:** 1:1

Crossover Epoxy

These products give you the best of both worlds: the clarity of an art epoxy plus the durability of a thick-set or **high-performance epoxy**. You can use them for everything from coating an art project to hang on the wall to creating deep river-style tables. They come with a catch though, of course. You can't pour them at more than ⅛ to ¼ inch at any given time. For a table or thick pour, that means layers. It might sound like a lot more work than one big pour, but you win when it comes to time. In a 12-hour day, I can do between two and four ¼-inch pours. That works out to up to 1 inch of epoxy in one day, which will cure enough to pour more the next day. With that math, you can pour and cure 2 inches in the time it takes to babysit a deep-pour or for a thick-set epoxy to cure. No BPA, low VOC, UV resistant.

BRAND: MakerPoxy by TotalBoat and Jess Crow

POT LIFE: 60–90 minutes

RATIO: 1:1

Casting Epoxy

A urethane or polyester resin, this type of epoxy creates great casts and **lathe** work. **Casting epoxies** love a **pressure pot** and give a crystal-clear finish to preserved flowers and other compact items. They don't work well for river-style builds or deep, long, wide pours. Not all casting epoxies are the same. Each manufacturer has a different set of rules for their formulas that you need to know and follow. Some cure best in a pressure pot or a **vacuum pot**, though some manufacturers advise against the latter. Because of their strength and clarity, you can turn casting epoxies, when properly cured, on a lathe and finish them either with polishing or a clear pour.

> **BRANDS:** ThickSet by TotalBoat, Clear Cast by Alumilite
>
> **POT LIFE:** 8–12 minutes
>
> **RATIOS:** 1:1, 2:1, some 3:1

Deep-Pour or Thick-Set Epoxy

These epoxies commonly go into **large pours** and tables. They can prove tricky to use, though, and not all are created equal. Some can pour at a maximum of 1 inch at a time, whereas other types must pour at a *minimum* of 1 inch. Read the **data sheet** carefully to know exactly what you're buying and make sure the product matches the project. As a liquid, these epoxies have crazy viscosity, so seal the **mold** completely. Otherwise, the epoxy will leak, even from a pinhole. Because of their viscosity, these epoxies need two to seven days to reach a **medium cure** and even longer for a **full cure**.

That long time frame also gives the liquid plenty of time to find its way onto your floor (and everywhere else) if you use anything less than a hermetically sealed mold.

> **BRANDS:** ThickSet and Fathom by TotalBoat, Amazing Deep Pour by Alumilite
> **POT LIFE:** 10–15 minutes, up to 60 minutes of work time
> **RATIO:** 3:1

High-Performance, Laminating, or Multipurpose Epoxy

These low-viscosity formulas work fantastically for laminating, **hand layups**, building layers, and bonding to fiberglass and other composite materials. They often resist moisture, too, making them ideal for use in boating, particularly surfboards, kayaks, and canoes. Some brands offer hardeners in varying speeds: fast, medium, or slow. For instance, if I was making a canoe in Alaska I would use High-Performance with the slow hardener. Why? Because the humidity in Alaska is very low and that would offer me enough time to work. However, if I were making the same canoe in Georgia, I would use the Tropical hardener to allow me a comparable work time within a high-heat, high-humidity environment. These hardeners all work with the same resin, but you absolutely cannot mix different brands of epoxy and hardeners. Variable-speed hardeners work interchangeably only within their own family line.

> **BRANDS:** High-Performance by TotalBoat, 105 Epoxy Resin by West System
> **POT LIFE:** 10–40 minutes
> **RATIO:** 2:1 or 3:1

Penetrating Epoxy

These ultra-low-viscosity formulas penetrate and seal wood. Used prior to a coating or thick-set epoxy, penetrating epoxy can help reduce bubbles and prevent checking, cracking, and rot. It also can stabilize punky wood, or soft rot. Use penetrating epoxy on clean, untreated wood. Mix only as much as you will use in a short amount of time and apply it immediately after mixing.

> **BRANDS:** Penetrating by TotalBoat, S-1 Clear Penetrating Epoxy Sealer by System Three
> **POT LIFE:** Less than 20 minutes
> **RATIO:** 2:1 or 3:1

Quick-Set Epoxy

Also called "fast-set" or "XX-minute," these epoxies function best for gluing and repair work and usually set within 2 to 15 minutes. They typically come in a two-part tube with a plunger that makes it easy to dispense **part A** and **part B** equally and simultaneously. Then, using a small stir stick, you can mix A and B together. They offer an extremely limited amount of time to complete your work.

> **BRANDS:** 4-Minute Epoxy by TotalBoat, ClearWeld by JB Weld, Instant Mix 5 Minute by Loctite
> **POT LIFE:** 1–15 minutes
> **RATIO:** Plunger packaged

UV Resin

UV resins contain one part resin only and don't require a stand-alone hardener to cure. For UV resin to cure properly, you need a **UV light apparatus or bar**. UV resin can cure in ambient sunlight, but it doesn't achieve a full cure as well or as quickly. UV resins can pour only in tiny increments, $\frac{1}{16}$ to $\frac{1}{8}$ inch, and they can't

EPOXY RESIN THICKNESS TABLE

THICKNESS (INCHES)	1:1 FORMULAS	2:1 FORMULAS	3:1 FORMULAS
$1/16-3/16$	✓	✓	✓
$1/8-3/8$	✓	✓	✓
$1/2-1$		✓	✓
$1-2$		✓	✓
$2-3$	✓ (urethane)	✓	✓
$6+$	✓ (urethane)		

cover large surface areas. These epoxies suit jewelry making and filling small holes or wood knots. Don't confuse UV resin with epoxies that contain UV inhibitors. These resins should come in black or lightproof bottles. Some formulas have a bothersome smell, according to some makers, so heed all safety measures before using them. UV resins also emit fumes and sometimes plumes as they cure.

BRANDS: TotalBoat, Let's Resin, Alumilite
POT LIFE: 6 months (unless exposed to UV light)
RATIO: n/a

Clear up any confusion about which epoxy is best for your project by using the table above.

AMOUNT OF EPOXY

There's an easy, simple tool to calculate how much epoxy you need for any given project: an Internet connection. Check out my free online calculator: JessCrow.com/epoxy-calculator. Enter the width, depth, and length of the epoxy project, and the calculator will give you a good idea of how much epoxy you need. No online calculators can account for the exact volume or mass of add-ins, such as toys, flowers, or flags, so adjust for those accordingly.

When working with a mold and a thick-set epoxy, you can use water. Yes, water. It not only gives you a good idea of how much epoxy you'll need, but it also automatically tests a mold for leaks, which you definitely want to avoid. Use a measuring cup to track the volume of water that you pour into the mold to the desired level. *Don't* use water if you're working with wood or another porous **substrate** because water will seep into those materials. Water works best with **HDPE** or silicone molds. You also need to be 100 percent positive that no water remains in the mold before you pour. It

must dry *completely*. Do the water test and any other calculations at least a few days prior to pouring.

If you can't access an online tool or use water to determine how much epoxy you'll need, be prepared to use leftover epoxy for other items, such as molds. It's always better to have more epoxy than less when pouring. If you run out midway and need to mix more, that scenario can create a perfect storm. If you already added color to the first batch, you'll face the challenge of matching the color of the second batch to the first. With pot life ticking down, you most likely will rush, and in your haste you could mix the second batch improperly. Even worse, once the first batch has begun its **exothermic reaction**, you might create an effect I call **seized** epoxy, which happens when you add a "cold" batch of epoxy to a warmer one. Again, it's always better to mix more epoxy than less and to use any leftovers to finish other projects or create small items, such as bookmarks or coasters.

COLORS

You'll learn more about color theory in the next chapter. This section covers color planning, which entails just one instruction. Write it down.

I love notebooks. I even have a favorite pen and write in *this* notebook only with *that* pen. My workbenches are black, so I can write on them with white, oil-based pens and keep notes on projects as I'm doing them. Epoxy peels right off Rite in the Rain paper. Mind blown.

Why am I telling you this? Because you need to keep good notes about exactly how much color goes into a project in case something goes sideways and you have to color-match it later. Keep track of how much epoxy a mold uses so you don't waste any the next time you use that mold. Take note of wood that didn't react well to a pour. You have endless reasons to keep a notebook handy, but recording color ratios is number one. Later you'll learn how to fix projects that do go sideways. To make those fixes,

you need to know exactly how much color you added to your epoxy.

Here's another good reason to keep notes on color. You mix 8 ounces of epoxy (parts A + B) and add 1½ teaspoons of **mica powder** to it, producing color X. To another 8-ounce cup of epoxy, you add 1 teaspoon of mica powder, which produces color Y. When you pour color Y at one end of a mold and color Y at the other, they meet in the middle and create the most epic color combo: color Z. Someone on social media sees your handiwork and wants to order 1,001 of those killer-colored objects to give to celebrities around the world, but they *all* must look just like the original. You never know when you may need to reference your color numbers, so always write them down.

You also need a dedicated set of measuring spoons or a scale, ideally both. Use those tools and record the information—every time—for future reference.

MOLDS

Premade molds come in sizes ranging from small rings to large tables. Smaller molds usually consist of silicone, whereas larger molds largely are made of **HDPE** or a similar material that can take the weight of a lot of epoxy.

Building your own molds offers a great way to bring your creativity to life. The shapes and options for tables, counters, and just about anything are endless. For example, you can use an object, laser, or computer numerical control **(CNC)** machine to cut a design into an acrylic panel. Then use casting silicone to create a mold from the object or custom-made acrylic design. You can use medium-density fiberboard **(MDF)** wrapped in **tuck tape** to create a small or large box. Using precut sections of MDF and screws, wrap the sections in tuck tape, assemble them with the screws, and seal them with silicone. This method takes a little bit more effort, but it also offers a fun introduction to building. You also can use a section of thin, flexible plastic such as **UHMW** or HDPE as the base. Use strips of UHMW or HDPE to create a round or oval shape, then affix the strips to the base with hot glue or silicone. Then pour directly onto the base section.

No matter which kind of mold you use, you must take care of it. Check it for leaks before every use. Clean it after every use and make sure it's flat when stored. If you made the mold from MDF, you may have to change the tuck tape after every use—or you might need to chuck it altogether if it sustained damage during screw removal and demolding.

If you use a mold purchased online or

locally—from Woodcraft, for instance—you might want to prep the mold with a **mold-release spray.** Lower-quality molds benefit from that treatment slightly more than taller, thicker, more professional silicone or HDPE molds. Either way, it never hurts to use a release agent, which will ensure that your epoxy releases easily and cleanly. The only drawback is planning. You need to plan ahead because the mold-release agent needs time to dry completely before you pour epoxy into it.

TIME

If you're working with an epoxy that has a 10-minute pot life, you have only 10 minutes to work before you have to commit to the outcome. If you're new to epoxy, the best way to avoid a lot of problems is to gather everything you need before you start pouring: **PPE**, cups, mixing utensils, tape, **heat gun** or **torch**, timer, additives, and anything else. Once you add part A to part B, you have only the time specified by the manufacturer to complete the pour. Proper preparation and planning will save you hundreds or even thousands of dollars and endless hours of stress and potential do-overs.

SEALANTS

If you have limited building experience, you might not grasp how porous all woods are. Sure, some are more porous than others, but all wood is porous to some degree. That statement also holds true for most organic compounds. Not prepping wood before a pour can cause endless bubbles and make it easy for epoxy to flow in all the wrong places. Epoxy loves to find microscopic holes in wood and make itself at home. This is where penetrating epoxy (page 38) shines. Because of its water-like viscosity, it dives in to every pore of the wood, locking itself

in and preventing the next epoxy that you want to use from producing bubbles.

If it's more cost effective, you can use the epoxy for your main pour to seal the wood. In that case, mix just enough epoxy to coat the wood, then use a **chip brush** or a similar disposable brush to brush the epoxy onto all the sections of wood that the main pour will hit.

EDGES

Deciding whether to tape the underside edge of a project, coat it in **liquid latex**, or leave it to drip over and then sand it off can feel like a daunting task. Some projects make it easy to decide that sanding is worth the time you'd trade for taping. A small coaster might take six minutes to tape and only four minutes to sand, whereas a large table might take 20 minutes to tape but *two hours* to sand. The situation gets a little more complicated when dealing with a complex shape. Picture a 6-inch wooden star. Sure, you can tape off the back, razor-cut the edges so the tape doesn't overhang, and then do your thing. You also could buy liquid latex from a costume store, quickly paint the underside of the star, allow it to dry, do your pour, and then simply roll off the liquid latex, which will take the epoxy drips with it like magic—or science . . . or both!

If you tape the underside of a project, here's a great way to remove the tape so it doesn't get stuck under the cured epoxy edge. Use your heat gun to gently heat the tape. For this method to work, you need to move fast for two reasons. First, you don't want to burn the tape. Second, you're warming the epoxy to soften it, but you don't want it to burn, either.

There's no universal answer to the question of which method to use for a given project. All these methods remove drips from the underside of your work using consumable products: tape, **sandpaper**, liquid latex. For me, the deciding factor is time. For one cutting board, I tape. For 250 cutting boards (which I'm doing now), I'm hitting them with my **double drum sander**.

WEIGHT AND SIZE

Keep in mind the weight and size of the finished object. If you're making a wall hanging, plan how to hang the finished item, which could weigh 20 pounds. Let's say you're making a table. Does someone need to carry it up four flights of stairs and down a narrow hallway? If so, will it fit around those corners, or do you need to design it in two sections? Always know

in advance when to go big or go home. In its liquid state, epoxy is heavy but not that heavy. Once it has cured, though, those pounds add up faster than all the food and drink you consume during vacation or the holidays!

If you're planning a large-scale pour, can you break it into two or three sections? If you can do two or three smaller pours, can you achieve the same results by using the Festool **domino joiner** or other methods of attachment? Many beginners don't know to consider these important aspects of large-volume pours, which can cause tremendous headaches. Do yourself a huge favor by calculating roughly how heavy an object might weigh when done.

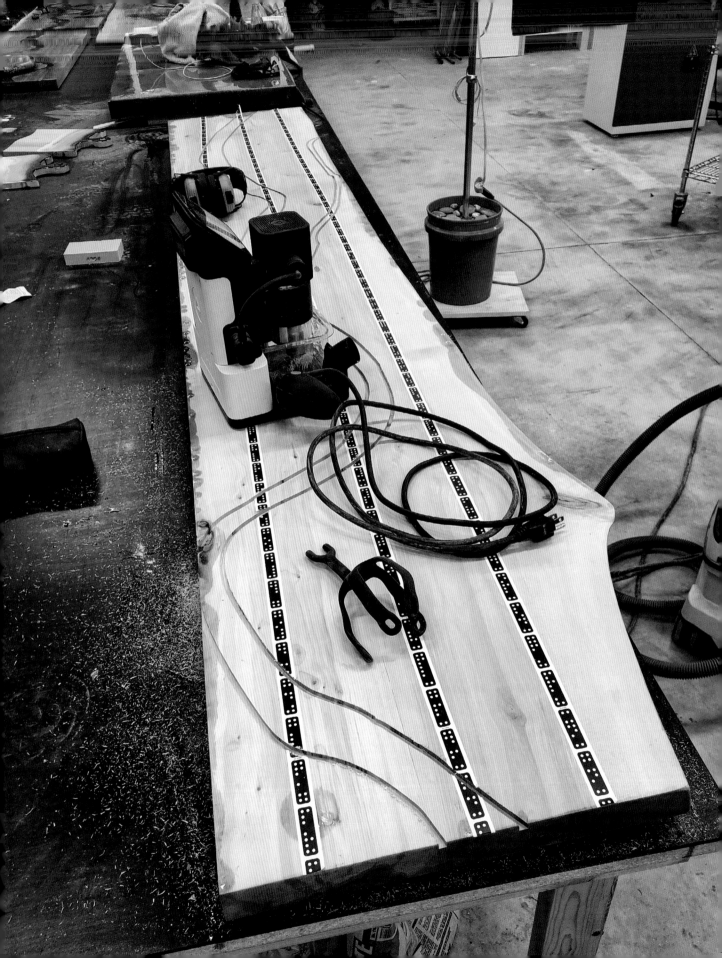

PART TWO

PROCESS MAKES PERFECT

5

MEASURE, MIX, COLOR, POUR

Great, Now It's on Fire

MEASURING

Before we address mixing, let's wade into the debate about weight versus volume, scale or measuring cup. Both sides swear that theirs is the only way to measure epoxy, but it's absolutely the manufacturer's call. Most producers have designed newer epoxies to be measured by volume. But some require a scale. If you're supposed to use a scale, don't forget to hit the tare button after you put your mixing cups on it. An incorrect **ratio** will prevent epoxy from curing properly. Also double-check that you've done the math correctly. Most epoxies measured by weight come in 2:1, 3:1, or higher formulas but give you the ability to do **casting** or thicker-volume pours.

If you measure by volume, don't use silicone measuring cups. They cure incorrectly, resulting in inaccurate measurements. My TotalBoat cups have tick marks on the side that measure the ratios directly. Almost all these cups have ratio marks near the lip of the vessel like these: 1:1:1, 2:1:1, 3:1:1, or 4:1:1. Some may even have a 5:1:1 ratio, but for most epoxies, you'll use less than a 5:1 formula. Before you plan a pour, familiarize yourself with the 1:1, 2:1, and 3:1 formulas.

Here's an example of how the cups work. Suppose you're using MakerPoxy, a **1:1 formula**. In that case, you pour **part A** to the desired line directly at the first 1 in the "1:1" column, then **part B** to the line directly at the second 1. A deep-pour or thick-set epoxy uses a 3:1 ratio. In that instance, you find the corresponding 3:1 grid and fill it with part A to the amount line that you need, let's say 4. Then, in the next column, you add part B to the corresponding 4. Always confirm that you're

using the right ratio for your epoxy and that you use the *same* amount number for each measuring column.

MIXING

You know that mixing makes for a successful pour, but how to mix?

In Atlanta, after one of my classes, one of my mentors came up to me. "I've never seen a room full of grown adults so mesmerized by watching someone mix something!" Brian (aka "Sedge") said, giggling with excitement and making wild arm movements. Not mixing correctly is one of the top three reasons for not achieving a successful epoxy project, so my students had good reason to pay close attention.

Move quickly but deliberately. You need to strike a balance between going fast enough to incorporate parts A and B but not so fast that you introduce bubbles into the mixture. If you add bubbles during this step, it's hard to get them out and they become part of the pour. Mixing with intention is paramount. If you're mixing a large batch, use a rubber flanged attachment on a drill (often called a paint mixer). But still go slowly. Don't choke the drill's trigger to full speed or, again, you'll introduce bubbles, which, depending on the type and brand of epoxy, will prove almost impossible to remove without a **vacuum pot** or **pressure pot**.

Whether mixing with a stick or a drill paddle, you need to fully incorporate part A into part B for the manufacturer's specified time. Scrape the sides and bottom of the mixing cup and, if working with a small cup, rotate it in your hand to incorporate any epoxy or hardener that might have stuck to the sides. If you see striations in your mixture, like inside a marble, you probably didn't do it correctly. You don't want to see anything that looks like oil and water in the mix. When mixed appropriately, your epoxy may

go from clear to cloudy to clear again. Maker-Poxy does this. When parts A and B make first contact, it looks clear; about two minutes into mixing it goes cloudy; then back to clear around the four-minute mark. This progression means you're doing it right.

Transfer freshly mixed epoxy into another container before your pour. It might seem like an unnecessary step, but it's a good idea because any unmixed epoxy or hardener likely has stuck to the sides and bottom of the mixing cup. A clean pouring cup increases your chances of not introducing uncured liquid into your pour.

COLORING AND ADDITIVES

Now that you've mixed your epoxy and hardener, it's time to add color. This is where my heart gets happy. Epoxy can work wonders with wood. It highlights the figure and character of a slab of walnut or hickory, and adding a deep purple hue to a section of ambrosia maple can make your work *pop*. The woodworking world hotly debates this practice, some folks firmly believing that adding epoxy to wood ruins it. If the epoxy work is done correctly, I disagree. It draws attention to the wood and all that it has to offer in a new way. You don't have to add color, but a touch of purple or brown can add an exciting element. If the color matches the wood, you'll never know it's there.

Add color *after* mixing the epoxy. If you add it before, you'll buck the ratios regardless of whether you're doing your calculations by weight or volume. Adding color after you've mixed your epoxy thoroughly ensures that other chemicals don't hinder it.

You can't use latex paint, colorants with high amounts of water (first ingredient), or oil-based **pigments**. You can work around some of these limitations, however. For instance, you could use latex paint between layers of epoxy, but test exactly what you want to do on a small sample board before proceeding to a **large pour**. Anything oil based will prevent epoxy from adhering to a **substrate**, so also keep that in mind as you plan your projects.

As you prep for a pour, note that some additives can get you into trouble. Additives designed for epoxy differ substantially from those that aren't. For example, bottles of lower-quality **liquid pigments** contain a lot of water to add volume. Water and epoxy don't play well together.

When you add color, use the 2 percent rule. Keep additives to less than 2 percent of working volume. You have a bit more wiggle room with **mica powder**, but the 2 percent rule holds firm for liquid pigments. If additives change the epoxy volume by more than 2 percent, you risk the epoxy not setting correctly.

You Get What You Pay For

If you've visited a local art or woodworking store recently, the prices of the high-quality pigments, dyes, or tooling probably astounded you in comparison to similar items at a big-box chain store. Art shops and woodworking stores sell lots of cost-effective items, but they also stock cream-of-the-crop items that embody the concept of "a little bit goes a long way."

One of the most fascinating phenomena I've witnessed as a teacher looks something like this: A student will spend $1,000 on wood or **molds**, $125 for a gallon of epoxy, and 89 cents on the color, the most visible element of the project! When water-saturated pigment causes the epoxy to seize or cure improperly, the question inevitably rises: "What did I do wrong?" Something that cost less than a dollar caused the problem. Falling head over heels for epoxy costs a lot of money, I know, and we all want to save money wherever we can. You've noticed that I've given you lots of tips on how to reduce expenditures—but quality pigment isn't one of them.

You have lots of options for coloring epoxy. My favorites include mica powders from Black Diamond Pigments and liquid pigments from MIXOL, Golden Fluid, and Liquitex. Dispersion pigments are thicker and heavier, akin to a paste or glue, and you need only a tiny amount to tint large quantities of epoxy. TotalBoat offers

an entire line of dispersion pigments that work beautifully, though not necessarily for painting directly on an object.

Also keep in mind that how a pigment looks in the bag or bottle doesn't always accurately reflect how it will look when mixed with the epoxy. Think of it this way: From an airplane, a lake might look rich and deep. But if you wade into it and scoop some of the water into your hands, it looks almost clear. It all boils down to depth and volume. In the container, the pigment is concentrated. In a clear epoxy, it will lose some of the depth it exhibits in the bottle. Consequently, the next sentence is very important.

Always add *less* pigment than you think you need. Always.

Why? Because it's always easier to add more pigment than to remove it. Because you can't remove pigment. You must mix more epoxy and blend it with the first mixture to get an even batch, hoping that the dilution looks OK. It's much more straightforward to add just one more drop of color or scoop of mica powder before pouring instead of having to mix another batch.

Color Theory

The concept of color theory can sound intimidating, but it's pretty simple once you take a look at it. On the next page is a standard color wheel. Warm colors (reds, oranges, and yellows) appear on the left, while cool colors (greens, blues, and purples) fall on the right.

When you work with more than one color at a time, you need to know just three basic principles: families, neighbors, and opposites, as illustrated below. Families stick together in varying shades of the same color, such as powder blue, royal blue, and navy blue. Neighbors have tones in common, achieving balance by standing next to each other, such as violet and purple. Opposites—called "complementary" colors in color theory because when combined they cancel each other out—create good contrast, such as purple and yellow.

Use the color wheel to plan your colorwork by first deciding which principle(s) you want to follow: families, neighbors, or opposites. Then draw lines connecting the colors you want to use. If the lines create a symmetrical shape—a straight line, balanced triangle, or rectangle/diamond—the color scheme will work. If not, the colors of your project will look unbalanced—which is totally OK if that's the effect you want to achieve.

If your favorite color is blue, consider using greens, violets, and oranges with it. If you dig red, go for purples, oranges, and greens as well. If you're not sure what you want, start with the colors of your substrate or embedded objects, such as stone, wood, or flowers. Those count, too!

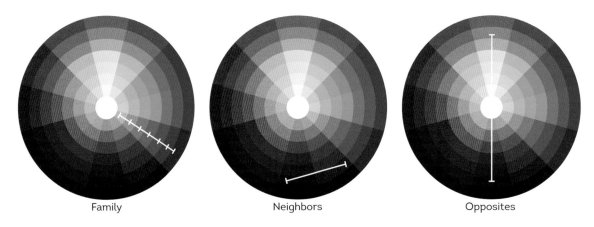

Family   Neighbors   Opposites

POURING

Sing it with me in your best 1980s hair-metal voice: "Pour epoxy on me!"

Just kidding. That's a bad idea! Always use PPE and avoid getting epoxy on yourself and others. But now that I have your attention, let's talk about how to decide whether to pour your epoxy all at once or in layers. When you're planning a project, it's not always clear which product will work best for your pour, whether a deep-pour epoxy such as ThickSet or a crossover epoxy such as MakerPoxy.

ThickSet has some benefits. You can pour 1 inch or more all at once, the color looks consistent because you can mix all your epoxy and color at the same time, and you have the freedom to walk away from your project for a few days while it cures. The downsides? ThickSet has viscosity like water, so you must use a mold or form, and it takes *days* to cure. It also uses either a 2:1 or 3:1 formula. MakerPoxy uses a 1:1 formula; it doesn't always require a form, you can pour multiple layers over 48 hours (that can total 1 inch or more), and it has enviable clarity. The downsides: MakerPoxy can't pour at more than $1/8$ to $1/4$ inch at a time, and if you want the same color throughout all layers, you must add color precisely to each batch. You also will use more gloves, cups, mixing devices, and other consumables.

I like working in layers because I'm impatient. Picture an angry badger. Give the badger an energy drink. Took the angry, caffeinated badger in a small room with an open set of finger paints and the prettiest white couch you've ever seen. My mind is that badger. I always am thinking about ideas, colors, ways to design things, and then ways to redesign them. My mind never sits still. It's always running laps, throwing color at everything. It gives me and folks like me a lot of creativity, but it also makes us super impatient—and explains why so many epoxy projects go sideways. When working with epoxy, patience is a verb. You can't rush. There's no way around it. With a few notable exceptions that we'll discuss shortly, you can't make the process go faster than it wants to go, and you can't force it into submission. That's why I use layers more often than thick-set pours.

In 48 hours, in the optimal environment, I can pour 10 layers of MakerPoxy to a finished depth of more than $1\frac{1}{4}$ inches. But sometimes ThickSet is the best, most effective way to pour a project. For a 30-foot table that requires a tremendous amount of epoxy, use ThickSet or Fathom epoxy not only for safety reasons—avoiding an accelerated **exothermic reaction**—but also for cost-effectiveness. For 100 percent color consistency, use ThickSet.

Want me to blow your mind? You can mix and match them.

Let's go back to that hypothetical 30-foot table. You want consistent color, but you also want to add objects to the pour. In this case, you'll use ThickSet to pour the main base layer. Build the mold, place the wood in it, seal the wood, check for leaks, add color to the Thick-Set, and do the pour. Before it cures completely, add the objects and allow the almost-cured ThickSet to act as a glue for those objects. Then use MakerPoxy for a final, clear **topcoat**. This strategy keeps the table safe for occasional food contact and protects the color and objects below the topcoat. A crossover epoxy such as Maker-Poxy cures faster than ThickSet, allowing you to finish your project sooner.

As long as you stay within the manufacturer's guidelines, you can approach an epoxy project in many ways. Be safe, don't waste money, and *try*. Explore new ideas and new techniques in new ways that work for you. Mix and match cured epoxy on a small scale and see what happens. The only rules you need to follow are the manufacturer's directions on ratios, mixing, and depth. Anything after that is fair game for creative, inspiring ideas and methods!

Smoking

You may have heard about or seen examples of epoxy projects or cups smoking. Scenarios like those are more common than I'd like to admit, but you can avoid them 100 percent by following this book closely and carefully. But why does epoxy sometimes smoke or go rock hard within seconds of pouring?

When you're prepping a pour, three commonplace errors can cause epoxy to smoke or **flash cure**:

1. You used the wrong type of epoxy, such as a large volume of high-performance epoxy instead of ThickSet for a deep pour.
2. You altered the ratios of part A and part B to speed up the curing process.
3. You added too many other items, such as liquid pigments, to the mixed epoxy.

If mixed epoxy starts to flash cure and smoke, immediately and *carefully* move the container, which could be *very* hot, to an open-air environment or open all available windows and external doors. Leave the area until the smoke has cleared.

If you try to speed the curing process by adding more part B or introducing a signif-icant, uncontrolled temperature variation, whether hot or cold air, you accelerate the exothermic reaction. Adding more hardener will speed nothing but a headache. The manufacturer's ratios are hard and fast rules, not guidelines. Variable-speed hardeners that come with specialty products such as Total-Boat High-Performance give you flexibility, but you can't add more hardener to the epoxy to make it cure faster.

My classes offer lots of suggestions for ways to work more efficiently. Sometimes that means a faster **cure time**. I occasionally will substitute ThickSet for a **high-performance epoxy**, with a huge caveat attached. You have to pour it in layers. I never pour a large volume of high-performance all at once, not because I don't want to but because *I can't*. Pouring a large volume of high-performance product will result in an accelerated exothermic reaction. Your project will go up in smoke along with your motivation to do more epoxy projects. It's imperative to pour it in small increments and work your way to the desired depth.

Hot boxes and curing boxes, like food dehydrators, act as enclosed ovens. They cure epoxy faster than the ambient air. They're great, but they need to have a stabilized temperature-control unit. (I've seen some wooden boxes with a **heat gun** attached and no temperature control to shut the heat gun off!) Never use a hot box or curing box that doesn't have a temperature-control mechanism and never leave it unattended. Doing so risks burning your epoxy and burning down your house or shop as well.

Familiarize yourself fully with how to use a hot box or curing box before using it on a last-minute, multi-pour project that a client expects tomorrow. Otherwise, you'll have to repurpose it like the projects in the pivoting and repurposing chapter (page 74).

6

SOLVING PROBLEMS

Bursting Your Bubbles

Now it's time to deal with bubbles, dust, bugs, and baby-sitting. Handling them is about as much fun as watching water not boil, but solving these problems, an extremely important step, also gives you an opportunity to ensure that the epoxy is curing properly and not getting too hot.

HEAT IT

We already touched on the Great Gun-Torch debate (page 32). Now let's dive a little bit deeper in to the subject. **Heat guns** manipulate epoxy. **Torches** pop bubbles. Yes, a heat gun can pop bubbles, but a torch can't manipulate epoxy. Some heat guns produce a lot of heat but little airflow, and vice versa.

Speaking of airflow, some folks swear by blowing on epoxy, like candles on a birthday cake. As you can imagine, that's a very bad idea. Why? You always should wear a respirator around curing epoxy, and you have to take off a respirator to blow on anything. That's the first no-no. Here's the second: Depending on the person, human breath contains 5 or 6 percent water vapor, the archenemy of epoxy, which blowing will spray all over your glorious project. Third reason: Have you ever tried to inflate an air mattress or water floatie by mouth only? You felt light-headed and winded after just a couple of minutes, right? Now imagine doing that up and down a 12-foot-long table filled with

6 gallons of epoxy. Three strikes; don't do it. You can place box fans on the ground to help circulate cooler air. Keep them low to the ground and make sure they *don't* blow directly onto your project, which can alter the rate at which the epoxy cures. The goal is to keep the air moving *around* the project but not *onto* the project.

Right, back to heat. Introducing heat to epoxy can accelerate the **exothermic reaction**. The amount of heat that a torch produces and its pinprick precision can cause the epoxy to gel prematurely and create burn spots. *Don't* use a heat gun if:

- You're **doming** (page 199).
- You're using a small **mold**, and the epoxy could spill from it easily.
- You don't want your epoxy to move and just need to burst the bubbles.

In those instances, use a torch.

If you're working with a thick-set epoxy, you don't need to manipulate it. In that case, a torch will get the job done without the hassle of a cord.

BUBBLES

Improperly prepped wood will invite a *lot of bubbles* to the party. Using a heat gun or torch to eliminate them only creates more. If you repeat the heat bubble cycle, your epoxy will start smolding and your wood will develop a burnt spot. Neither one is a good look. Before you dump your supplies and say goodbye to your new epoxy friends online, remember that you probably didn't prep the wood correctly. Mixing can introduce *some* bubbles, but if a relatively bubble-free mix starts fizzing—prompting curses and tears—look to the **substrate**.

Adding more heat will make it worse. Heat makes wood swell in a process called **thermal expansion**, which allows *more* air to enter the wood. So find a good balance between using heat to eliminate bubbles and not using it to compensate for poor preparation. Not understanding or coming to terms with that balance will cause headaches and can ruin a project.

When you use a torch or heat gun to pop bubbles, hold the heat over the section with bubbles for microseconds. As soon as you wave either tool over the epoxy, the bubbles will dissipate. Allow the epoxy to cool back down before introducing more heat.

COVER VERSIONS

You've prepped your substrate, mixed the epoxy perfectly, added just the right amount of colorant, and your pour looks perfect. Then, as you admire your handiwork, a fleck of dust falls right into it. Horror descends as you panic-calculate how much more dust is clinging to the joists above . . . just as the kids start a dance party upstairs. Ah, life.

Solution: You need to use protective coverings for your projects while they cure. The absolute

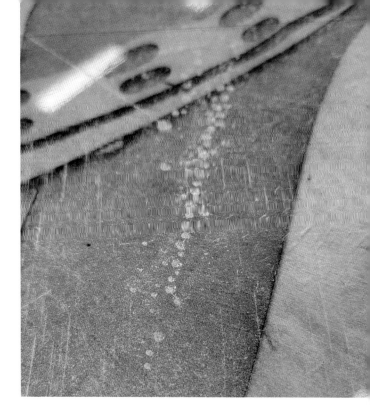

best way to keep dust off your project is to create a finish room. My shop has a room dedicated solely to epoxy pours. The large, brightly lit space has an air filter to pull the air from the room. The lights shine at multiple angles, which helps reduce glare and also highlights any defects in the pour. Tightly sealing doors separate the room from the rest of my shop. No sanding takes place in that room, nor any other activity that might bring dust into it. For years, though, I worked in a small, one-car garage shared with vehicles, a snowblower, scampering kiddos, and the occasional shedding dog. To mitigate the particulate that can find its way into just about any setting, here are some easy ways to protect your work.

Use totes. For a small item, flip a rubber or plastic tote over it while curing.

Build a plastic tent. Suspend a rope above your work area, drape plastic sheeting over it, and pull it open when working and closed when not, like a shower curtain in reverse. A plastic tent makes a great solution for shared spaces and **large pours**.

Use a collapsible spray-paint booth. You can find these portable shelters at your local hardware store. Some fold into small, easy-to-store packages when not in use.

Modify these options to fit your space and situation. If you live in an apartment, you probably aren't working on a 12-foot table, so a tote or small paint booth will help protect your projects. If you're working in your garage, install a pulley system with rope and a plastic tarp that you can move when you want to use the garage for parking a vehicle.

BUGGING OUT

A few years ago, a client commissioned me to make a table that incorporated lily pads, koi, and other natural elements that you might see in a pond or slow-moving stream. The table took almost two months to complete. Painted in four or five painstaking layers, the lily pads created such a convincing illusion of depth that it felt like you could reach into the

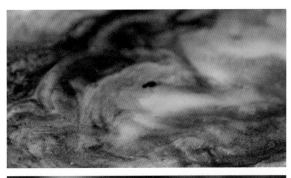

water and touch them. The scales of the hand-painted koi shimmered when the light hit them just right.

About three or four weeks after the client took the table home, a text message popped up on my screen: "Don't worry about it, the kids think it's cool."

Huh?

Then a picture slowly loaded . . . to reveal a fly *in* the table!

During the final portion of the pour, a fly (obviously) had landed on the build. I always keep an eagle eye on my epoxy while pouring, so it had to have happened at the end of the gel state. The fly had sunk into the epoxy, *Jurassic Park*–style, completely encased with its wings intact, beady little eyes staring back at me, mocking me. I offered to collect the table and remove the little bugger from what instantly became one of the most embarrassing client jobs I'd done. But nope—they loved it and opted to keep the fly forever encased in their table: a great talking point for anyone who noticed.

But what if you don't want a fly to call one of your tables its forever home? What if a gnat lands on your work while it's still in the gel state? If your epoxy is still in the gel phase *at all*, use fine-tipped tweezers or a gloved hand to remove the offending insect or particulate. If you're using a **self-leveling** epoxy such as MakerPoxy, a quick flash of your heat gun will soften the spot. Blast it with a wide, sweeping motion to soften *all* the epoxy in the area, which will ensure that it all smooths out properly.

If you're using a thick-set epoxy, you may have to use needle-nose pliers or another tool to reach the sunken invader. The stage at which your epoxy is curing will dictate how much time you have to remove the annoyance as well as how much *delicate* heat you'll need to flatten the epoxy again. I know, I said you shouldn't use the heat gun or torch too often or it'll **toast** the epoxy and might accelerate the exothermic reaction. You won't find much discussion of this gnarly situation on social media. Nevertheless, it's a critical "proceed with caution and don't burn it" moment that you need to understand and negotiate safely.

If you're so far into curing that you can touch the epoxy without your gloved hand getting sticky or if the epoxy behaves like taffy in the sun—hard but pliable—remove the bug or particulate, and you *still* can introduce heat with a heat gun, *not a torch*. This method works best with a self-leveling formula, such as MakerPoxy, which helpfully features an extended work time. Proceed with *extreme* caution if using other epoxies.

Here's the three-step process.

1. Make sure your space is as ventilated as possible and you have your respirator on properly.
2. Using tweezers or whichever tool will do the job, dig out the foreign object, removing as much of it as possible. Consider this a one-time procedure. You can make matters worse if you have to go in again.
3. Set your heat gun to low and pretend you're spray-painting. Make broad, sweeping motions across the whole area from which you pulled the object. Focus not only on that specific area but also on the wider section around it.

Spreading the heat softens the epoxy, allowing it to fill in the void you created when you pulled out the foreign object. Again, this step is necessary only if you absolutely must remove something while the epoxy is *still malleable*. In most cases, you can remove the annoying invader threatening to ruin your project and close any gap formed during the removal process.

BABYSITTING

Babysitting isn't just for teenagers looking to make some cash. Keeping an eye on your project is one of the necessary steps to ensure a successful pour. Walking away from any pour in a fresh stage can cause hours of frustration and wasted money. Confirm the epoxy has set up enough to be left alone and is doing what you want it to do, meaning, for example, that it isn't spilling from the mold. Thinking, *Eh, I'm sure it'll be fine* will guarantee that it won't by extending an invitation to Murphy and his law to join the party.

When planning a pour, account for time. Don't do a large-scale pour if you have to run out the door for a soccer game in 30 minutes or when you're having guests for dinner in an hour and you think you can fit in *just one more pour* on that table. Don't do it.

Instead, allot time for prepping, pouring, and babysitting. It will save you time and peace of mind in the long run. Not watching your work carefully can result in embedded bugs and dust, epoxy all over the floor, and many more unpleasant, costly errors. The amount of time you need depends on the type of epoxy you're using. Epoxy with a short cure time requires minimal babysitting. Epoxy with a long cure time needs more watching.

7

MOLDS AND EDGES

Take It All Off!

Now it's time to tackle how to wrest your project from its **mold** without ruining it and how to clean up those annoying underside drips.

REMOVING THE MOLD

You can manage smaller molds more easily than larger ones, but little ones can prove just as frustrating when epoxy sticks to them. You've learned about mold prep and how to plan properly to prevent a lot of basic errors (page 41). That preparation will help make demolding a whole lot easier.

For a pliable mold, removing it looks relatively straightforward. Once the epoxy has cured, twist and turn the mold until the project pops out. But what happens if your mold has a minor defect and the epoxy has stuck to it? Move slowly and carefully around the sticking point to release the surrounding epoxy. Depending on the location, carefully use the edge of a razor blade, putty knife, or other small, flat tool to pry the mold from the epoxy. Take care not to damage the mold or your epoxy work. If you can't reach the area where the mold has stuck—say, the bottom center of a tray-style mold—flip the mold upside down and let gravity have a go at it. If all else fails, you may have to sacrifice the mold to save the project.

If using a rigid mold—made from **MDF** and **tuck tape**, for example—you need to reverse-engineer the mold to remove it. Once the epoxy has cured fully, remove the last screw first and work your way around your mold. Here's yet another example of how writing and drawing in a physical notebook can help: You can sketch exactly how you assembled the mold so you know how to reverse the steps. If any edges stick to the epoxy (and they often do), use a rubber mallet to whack the MDF away from the project, remaining mindful, again, not to damage the epoxy work. For a little extra protection, lay a thin blanket or cloth over the appropriate section of the epoxy before using the mallet.

If you're using an **HDPE** or **UHMW** mold, epoxy simply won't stick to it. My workstations are made from those plastics, which also prove exceptionally durable. For the best bang for your buck, HDPE or UHMW molds and workbenches will outperform and outlast silicone or MDF all day long, even if they cost more up front. Over time, they more than pay for themselves because you won't have to go through the exercise and expense of constantly making MDF molds, which you often can't use again, or using silicone molds that ding, scratch, and warp.

CLEANING EDGES

You already learned how to plan for dealing with drips (page 42) and other ways to reduce epoxy buildup on the underside of your projects. But you still have to remove them.

If you taped your edges, try one or both of the following options. Use your **heat gun** to gently warm the tape and the epoxy and then pull the tape off. This trick works nicely and often results in a satisfying sensory moment as you watch little drips of epoxy pop across your workspace. Make sure small animals or children don't get to them before you clean them up. Using your heat gun also creates a sharp edge most of the time. Don't use so much heat that you burn the epoxy, though. Just warm the tape and drips, then pull. Babysitting also works. As you go on your epoxy journey, you'll notice the nuances of how epoxy and your workspace interact. In my shop, approximately four hours after a tabletop pour, I can peel the tape gently from the underside of the table because the epoxy has cured enough to form a small curl or dome but not enough to need heat or another method to remove it. It works best when the epoxy enters the "taffy" state described earlier, hard but pliable, but hasn't cured fully. This method is specific to workspace environment (temperature, water content of air) and epoxy (type, desired tackiness), so tread carefully. Only you can figure out the right time frame in your pouring location to support this method.

If you didn't use tape or **liquid latex** and the epoxy has cured fully, you need to sand the drips. If you're not familiar with sanders or sanding, spend some quality time at your local hardware store, which has an abundance of sanders, and familiarize yourself with them. Select the best **orbital**, **disc**, or **finish sander** you can find, heeding how it fits in your hand. Why? Because you'll be using it *a lot*. Your hands will thank you for buying an efficient

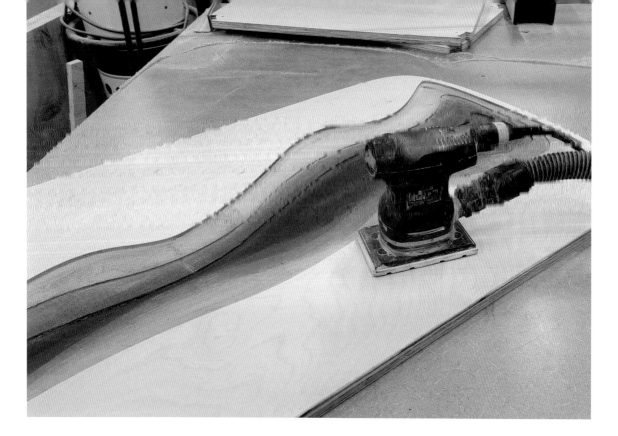

sander that fits well in your grasp. A sander truly can make or break a project in its final stages. You'll learn more details about sanding in the next chapter, but for now let's focus on how to sand underside drips without ruining the work on top.

Flip It and Reverse It

First arrange a cushioned or padded surface that supports the whole project. Scratching or dinging the hard work you just finished will ruin your day, I promise. Let's use a table to illustrate how to sand drips from the underside effectively.

Flip your table onto the cushioned surface. Start with 60-grit **sandpaper** and work your way around the edge of the table *once*, using only the weight of the sander as pressure to grind the drips. Then load your sander with 120-grit sandpaper and repeat the process. The next steps depend on how you want to finish your project. If you're using a product such as

Rubio Monocoat or ProCoat UnoCoat, which protects wood in a single layer, stop sanding at 120 grit for the entire project. You'll have to read the directions for further guidelines. But if you're using a finishing product that requires sanding up to 400 grit, start at 60 and progress through 80, 120, 180, 220, 320, and so on until you achieve the desired results.

8

SANDING AND FINISHING

The End Is Near!

Deciding whether to sand your epoxy represents the final step of a good pour and the light at the end of the tunnel. In this chapter, you'll learn whether to finish with more epoxy, another type of finish, or nothing at all. It all depends on the goal for your project. First you need to answer two questions about your project, which encapsulate the most important concerns in this chapter:

1. Will you serve food on this build?
2. Have you used the finishing product before with long-term results?

FOOD FOR THOUGHT

When I was learning about epoxy, I had limited access to limited information: social media from the art world and sometimes confusing **data sheets** that people rarely discussed. That was about it. Going with the crowd, I didn't even do much of my own research. River-style tables were becoming trendy at that time, but no one was talking about their durability or food safety. You either loved the style or hated it. Again, that was about it. Now you can find a plethora of river tables, countertops, and serving boards, all made from epoxy, and the conversation about them has broadened to include controversial topics, including food safety.

The guidelines from the U.S. Food and Drug Administration (FDA) begin: "Resinous and polymeric coatings may be safely used as the **food-contact surface** of articles intended for use in producing, manufacturing, packing, processing, preparing, treating, packaging, transporting, or holding food"—hey, good news!—and continue for another 11,000 words (oof). Broken-record alert: You really should read the whole document. Most of it boils down to a simple sentence: Almost all resins, regardless of mixture, when allowed to cure *properly*, are **safe for contact with food**. It's mission critical to keep those two specifications in mind. No colorants and no skipping steps. A proper cure doesn't mean "hard to the touch" or "it hasn't felt tacky for three days." It means a complete cure according to the manufacturer's data sheet. Do your research and always educate yourself about any product *before* you use it or expose others to it.

PEELING

Nope, it's not just for sunburns.

A few years ago, a great project gave me a "Hey, I made that!" moment. I had just finished a beautiful 10-foot table with my version of the Kenai River running through it. The icy blues of the captivating, glacier-fed river embody the beauty of Alaska. I had worked hard to capture its colors in a large walnut table. It turned out beautifully . . . until, a few days later, I noticed a small fleck on the surface.

At first, it seemed like something that might have fallen from the ceiling in the garage, where I'd been working. Further investigation revealed, to my complete horror, that the finish was *peeling*. When you see something peeling, the proper response is to peel it up some more (ugh). That little fleck heralded a weeklong process of pulling up the varnish.

The finishing product I'd used didn't adhere to the table properly. The varnish had stuck to *some* sections but not all of them, giving the whole project a mottled, sunburned look, and the remaining varnish gummed up the **sandpaper** on my sander.

That week retaught me a valuable lesson. *Test all finishes.* In the end, all the varnish came up, and I sealed the table properly. But relearning that lesson cost me two weeks and thousands of dollars. Running a sample section first might have taken a day and cost $40 total. Wasting money is one thing, but you can't recoup lost time.

SANDING

If you want a matte look and feel for your project, you most likely will sand it. Here are some other reasons to sand:

- The epoxy didn't level properly. For instance, a tabletop set unevenly.
- The project has drips on the top, sides, or bottom.
- A multisided project required multiple pours, causing multiple planes of drips.
- A fly landed in it (ahem).
- An error resulted in a divot or other deviation.

If you're going to do a **flood coat**, it's typical to stop sanding with 120- or 220-grit sandpaper. But what happens if you accidentally over-sand? In Alaska, where I live, windshield chips happen all the time in the fall, when the roads ice and trucks sprinkle them with pebbles. If the chip is small enough, you take it to a roadside stand and have the chip fixed then and there. The stands inject resin into the chip, and you're on your way (to get another chip). Fixing sanding scratches works the same way, but it works well only if you're going to add a flood coat.

If you're *not* planning to add a flood coat, keep sanding until you remove all marks from the sander or sandpaper. To achieve a uniform, swirl-free finish, keep increasing the sandpaper **grit size**, as stated previously, until you reach the desired sheen. You also can use a handheld buffer with a polishing compound, such as TotalBuff by TotalBoat, to buff the epoxy, much as you'd buff a car. Given enough time, buffing can give epoxy a mirrorlike finish. But note an exception to this rule. If you're using a high-end **finishing oil**, follow the manufacturer's instructions about exactly which sandpaper grit to use. Some recommend sanding wood projects to a maximum grit of 120 and then applying the oil.

FLOOD COATS

Will your project contact food? If so, a flood coat will help make you a responsible maker. To protect yourself and others, take the time to do a flood coat on any project that you expect to have even passing contact with food, either by using an epoxy that has been deemed **safe for occasional food contact** or a similar finishing product that states it is **food safe**. Many great products out there are "food safe," but not all of them will adhere to the epoxy you're using. Some will wipe right off, rendering them useless, so go for one that will bond to epoxy (or wood), providing long-term durability and safety.

You may want to do a flood coat for other reasons. For example, you may have sanded a project to level it, and now you want to do a flood coat of clear epoxy to restore the original shine. Maybe you had to sand a piece to remove a fly. Flood coats ensure that your projects are level, protected, and shiny. Some folks prefer sanding their projects to a high gloss instead of doing a flood coat, and that works well, too. For me, it's all about time. Flood coats often take less time than high-gloss sanding or a buffing finish.

OTHER FINISHES AND TOPCOATS

Lots of great finishing oils and **topcoats** offer an array of finishing sheens, from glossy to matte and everything in between. Some of these products adhere to epoxy wonderfully, but others merely skim the coat, resulting in a temporary finish. Choosing the right product for your project will result in a long-term protective coat.

Some all-natural products come from plants, nuts, and even bugs. The following examples are safe for food contact when fully cured or inert:

- beeswax
- carnauba wax
- mineral oil
- pure tung oil
- raw linseed oil
- shellac
- walnut oil

But some won't stick to every type of epoxy, so double-check before you buy. If you're still not sure, always run a test.

Hybrid finishes like ProCoat Uno Finish, Rubio Monocoat, and Osmo combine wax and oil to protect. Of course you can use dyes, lacquers, and varnishes to finish wood. All these products have different brand names, too numerous to list here, but specialty stores such as Woodcraft carry the hybrid finishes and all others. Big-box stores carry an array of lacquers, stains, and varnishes but typically don't carry hybrid finishes. Again, always sample or test the finish *before* applying it to your whole project. That's the only way to know *for sure* that it will work.

UV AND THE GREAT OUTDOORS

To date, no epoxy on the consumer market is fully UV retardant. Some products (MakerPoxy, for instance) contain UV inhibitors, and some products can protect the surface of your project from UV light. But right now no epoxy will protect your project from it 100 percent. It's worth repeating—yes, again—that UV resin is *not* epoxy containing UV inhibitors. Pay close attention to wording on labels.

When planning a project, think long and hard about where your project will live when done. If

it's going outside, you need to add a layer or two of Halcyon varnish or a similar product. If it's going in a room that gets lots of direct sunlight, the colors will fade over time.

Case in point. A while back, one of my students asked me a question. He acted a bit timid about showing me pictures of his project because he clearly felt like the only person in the world who had ever made a mistake. After I reminded him that I've made a ton of them myself, he showed me a photo of a table that he'd finished. It was half blue and half green—and not on purpose. The client was upset and my student was at a loss because, he said, he'd used the same epoxy and **pigment** all at the same time. Theoretically nothing should have gone wrong.

Some investigating literally brought to light that half the table had spent its daylight hours basking in the California sun. All that UV exposure had accelerated yellowing. Half the table had gone green because blue + yellow = green. My student learned the hard way that he should have used UV protectant on the table. Keep that lesson in mind as you move forward with large builds and use as much forethought as you can about your project to sidestep avoidable problems like this one.

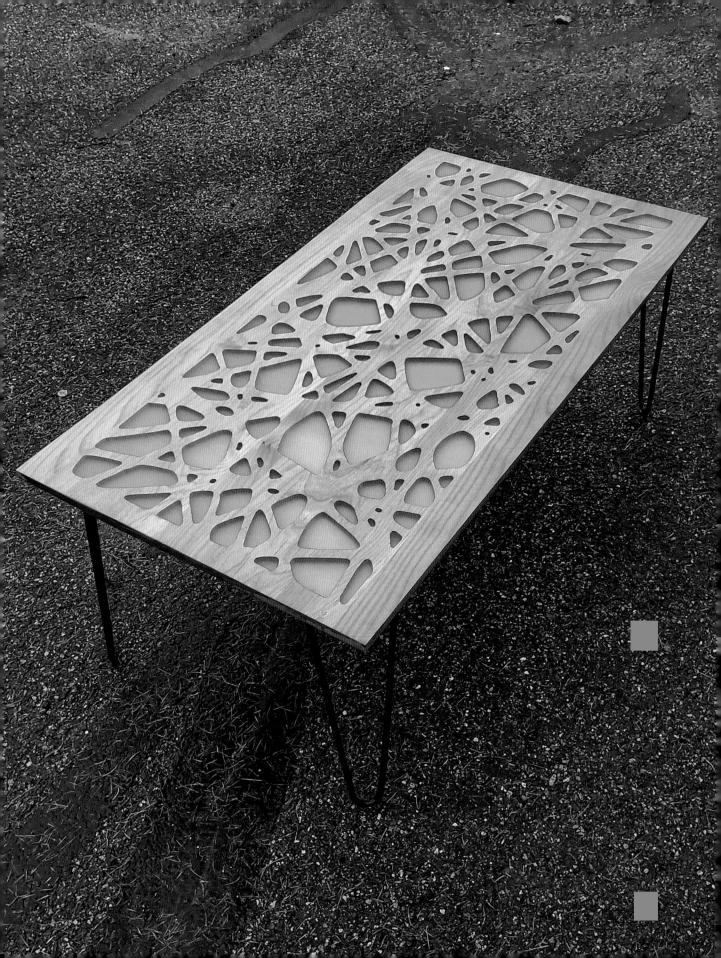

PART THREE

NO GOING
BACK

9

REPAIR AND MAINTENANCE

Easy Button, Ugh Button

Even when you've done everything correctly, some things—errant dust, flies bent on self-destruction—lie beyond your control. But learning how to handle the slips that epoxy life throws at you will help you complete your journey. Let's learn how to fix some of these inevitable blips and maintain your project over time.

BUGGING OUT . . . AGAIN

In the anecdote that I shared in the solving problems chapter (page 53), my clients didn't want me to remove the fly. But if they had chosen otherwise, I had a few options to get rid of it. These two fixes apply *only* to fully cured epoxy. If your project hasn't cured all the way yet, go back to that chapter, which specifically deals with uncured epoxy.

If you've kept your color work toward the bottom of your project, with clear epoxy toward the top section—where most blunders happen—repairs will prove much easier. Keep that in mind when planning a project. Keeping color low and clear epoxy high is easier to fix, and it works for food contact.

If you spot a small bug or other foreign object, including dust, in your cured epoxy and it lies close to the top of the project, you can use a drill with a bit that matches the size of the offending object you're trying to remove. Don't drill too far into the **substrate**, though, lest you punch *through* it. That's why I prefer to use a razor blade to carve out the object manually. A razor blade or craft knife gives you more control over how much epoxy you remove. It also allows you to carve out the object in a funnel shape, using the razor head as a pivot point. After you remove the object, clean out any particulate. You may need to use **sandpaper** to soften the edges of the funnel-shaped hole, depending on the size of the object removed. To finish cleaning up, use a cotton swab or small brush dipped in denatured alcohol to remove any leftover residue. Allow the alcohol to dry completely before moving to the next step.

A lot of variables can come into play when deciding how to handle a repair. Is your project fully poured, meaning that it has a fully cured **topcoat**? Does the top layer contain color? Did you sand the entire object to a matte finish? Is the foreign object a few layers down? All the possible variations would run for pages and pages. So let's look at two scenarios for when an unwanted object has found its way into your fully cured epoxy work. Hopefully they'll help you resolve the issue.

Scenario 1

You have a fully poured 2-inch-deep table with artwork and color in the first three layers. Above that there is one ¼-inch layer not altered in any way, ensuring proper **food-contact safety**. The fly sank somewhere between the last layer of artwork and the top layer of epoxy, fully encased, mocking you with its beady little eyes. You remove the little bugger, then patch the hole with a small amount of new epoxy. Apply a drop of the patch epoxy, allow it to cure, then buff the area to match the rest of the table.

When thinking about how best to remove an object, consider two options:

- spending time and money on buffing compound, pads, and elbow grease to bring all of it back up to a shine
- spending time and money on more cups, epoxy, and waiting for the table to cure again

I would choose the second option.

If you use a **self-leveling** epoxy, such as MakerPoxy, you don't even need to fill in the hole; the epoxy will do that for you—and hold the same level across the whole table.

Once the repair is complete, keep the table under a plastic tent or stand guard to make sure that nothing else causes further issues!

Scenario 2

This type of repair can prove more difficult, especially if you didn't keep your colorwork ⅛ or, better yet, ¼ inch below the topcoat of clear epoxy. Keeping colorwork below the topcoat ensures food-contact safety and avoids the near-impossible task of color-matching the existing epoxy with a new batch.

Here's the scenario. You've created a table in a **mold**, using two slabs of wood. Colored epoxy fills the void in the center of the table between the two slabs. You've sanded it fully and treated it with **finishing oil**. But then you notice a large particle of dust or lint in the table, in the top layer of the epoxy under the finishing work and oil. Because you used finishing oil, pouring a new, full topcoat of epoxy won't work for aesthetic reasons and because that new layer might not adhere properly.

In this case, you remove the dust or lint with a razor or drill, clean out the divot, and prepare the area. But here comes the hard part. You didn't keep the color low, so you have to color-match. In the effective planning chapter (page 34), you learned about writing down exactly how much color you added to precisely how much epoxy in case something like this situation happens. So you mix another batch of epoxy, using the same color ratio as the initial pour. This step might result in a perfect match . . . or it might not. Color-matching can prove particularly challenging with epoxy because it's a finicky medium. Fill the hole with the new colored epoxy and allow it to cure fully. Once again, fully cured *doesn't* mean hard to the touch. It means cured according to the manufacturer's guidelines. When the epoxy has cured, resand the entire table and recoat it with the finish of your choice. Sometimes you can resand just the section in question but not always. Prepare for the worst and hope for the best.

Keep in mind a few additional notes. If you can't color-match the section, you may need to sand or plane the *entire* table to get rid of the offending object. Hopefully it needs only a few passes of a sander or planer. Even if it does, this step takes a lot of extra time and money. A clear topcoat always gives you more flexibility and rules out having to color-match. Always exercise diligence when removing finishes. If any finish remains and you recoat the project, expect even more headaches if the new finish doesn't adhere to the old one.

CHIP REPAIR

Like everything else, this situation has an "easy" button solution and an "ugh" button solution. An easy solution might simply entail adding a small amount of epoxy to a small ding. Not so easy if you have to color-match, sand, and recoat. The approach you take depends on the size of the chip. Always start by adding a small amount of epoxy. If that doesn't work, go back to Bugging Out . . . Again and the two possible scenarios.

You also can fix small chips with UV resin. You can tint it, it cures almost instantly with a **UV light bar**, and it makes small repairs durable. Another way to fix a small chip is to sand the area around it lightly, which will soften the edges. If the chip is small enough, not very deep, and in a location that isn't a deal-breaker, lightly sand enough to remove the chip, then reapply the sealing finish. If that's a finishing oil, easy-peasy. If you sealed it with a full epoxy pour, you're going to need to use more elbow grease.

Keeping these scenarios in mind and actively thinking, *What's the worst that can happen?* because it *will* happen—will make you a better artist, builder, or maker and save you a lot of aggravation.

FADING

Remember that California blue-green table? Yellowing and fading can happen to anything you make: a countertop, wall art, even a charcuterie board. Projects exposed to lots of sunlight year-round (not Alaska) will yellow and fade faster than in less sunny places (Alaska). The best way to avoid fading is to apply a UV protectant. I use Halcyon varnish, but you can find other options on the market. Whatever you choose, always test it *before* you apply it to an entire project and send it out into the world.

Whichever product you use, you'll need to recoat it every six months to a year or tell a client which product to use and when. Small care cards are great for exactly this reason. I also tape my business card under projects for clients so they easily can reach me if they have any questions or need recommendations for products to use.

CLEANING

Don't use harsh chemicals on your epoxy projects, especially tables or counters, which see a lot of use. The best cleaning method is plain old soap and water. That's it. Products containing alcohol will degrade epoxy over time, and harsher chemicals can leave your work feeling sticky or, as one student described it, like a cat's tongue. Vinegar-based products have been getting traction for deep cleaning, but I haven't used them enough on my own work to recommend them without reservation. Again, use caution when using any surfactant containing acid or alcohol, which could cause the epoxy to degrade.

10

PIVOTING AND REPURPOSING

But It's Still Sticky!

Life happens. When you've made a significant error in bringing your project to fruition, you need to master the skill of pivoting. This chapter will share some of the worst-case scenarios and the important lessons you should learn from them. Confronting those *What's the worst that could happen?* thoughts and understanding how to repurpose or redo will give you something you can't buy at a store: hope. Will the project turn out the way you envisioned at the beginning? Maybe not. But it also could become something even better.

EPOXY AND PUPPIES

A project that has cured only partially or not at all can bring you as a maker to the breaking point in so many exciting ways. Spending days, weeks, or even months on a project that has cost a lot of money but not cured fully can prove extremely frustrating.

It may seem obvious, but here's a quick story about why having puppies around epoxy is a terrible idea. For more than a month, I worked on a 4-by-8-foot countertop, a stunning Kenai River beauty in birch. While I was at it, I thought it would be a good idea to bring home not one but *two* puppies. To keep them safe while I worked in the garage, they stayed in the house. For keeping tabs on them, however, the garage door stayed cracked open. Just as I was mixing 2 gallons of epoxy for the protective **topcoat**, Astrid, my little destroyer, nuzzled the door open and ran happily through the garage. As you and I both know, it's never safe to have small pets around uncured epoxy. Panic ensued as I frantically tried to set aside the epoxy; take off my respirator, gloves, and goggles; and not make a bigger mess than I already had made while trying to wrangle a happy-go-lucky pup and then, oh no, her equally troublemaking sister, Ophelia. Both puppies came barreling up to me, right over epoxy drips that had been pooling on the garage floor all day. I managed to get them inside safely and, because MakerPoxy has

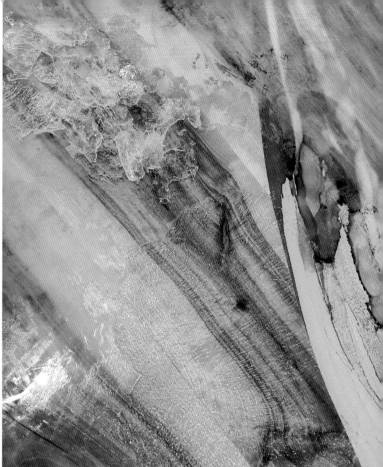

a 60-minute **pot life**, I still had time to complete my pour.

But.

The next morning, half of the counter had cured as it should have, but the other half still looked straight-up gooey. Two choices presented themselves: troubleshoot the entire project into the trash or find a way to save it. Ah, puppies.

The only way to deal with an error like the one I just described, should you encounter it, is to remove the uncured epoxy. Use lots of denatured alcohol or a similar product specifically labeled "epoxy remover," plenty of paper towels, and several heavy-duty trash bags. Once you've donned your **PPE**—industrial rubber gloves, respirator, goggles—pour the alcohol or cleaning product onto the uncured section and allow it to sit until it becomes easy to scoop out the uncured epoxy. This time frame depends on the amount of epoxy to be removed and the variability of which sections remain fully or partially uncured. The product essentially is dissolving the bonds of the epoxy and hardener, so give it as much time as you can to do the hard work. Scoop up the uncured mess and dispose of it in your trash bags. Repeat until you've removed all the uncured epoxy and hardener. Remember to take the trash bags to the hazardous waste section of your local dump. *Don't include the bags with your regular garbage.* Yes, we talked about this in the proper protection chapter (page 23), but it's worth reiterating. Uncured epoxy and hardener and paper towels soaked with them are toxic to humans, animals, and the environment.

You also need to peek under the cured epoxy. To do so without causing (more) damage, use a small stir stick, chisel, or other flat, dull tool to carefully lift an edge of the cured epoxy. If it doesn't budge, breathe a sigh of relief through your respirator. The epoxy cured properly. But if it lifts easily and you can see uncured epoxy beneath the surface, you'll have to start chipping away at it. In my case, it took three full hours to pull up all the half-cured epoxy with a chisel.

When faced with a problem like that, a lot of my students ask, "Why don't you just sand it?" Seems like an easy way to deal with it, but have you ever tried to pull a big wad of chewed gum from your hair or someone else's? Uncured or partially cured epoxy will gum up a sander or planer faster than you can blink. You'll waste an unbelievable amount of **sandpaper** or planer blades if you try to take that shortcut.

But once you've removed all the uncured epoxy, you should use your sander. Start with 80 grit and smooth the exposed section. In this step, you want to feather the epoxy that remains. Once you have it roughly shaped, work your way through higher grits, as described previously (page 61). Make sure to scuff the cured epoxy to give those areas something to hold on to for the next step.

When you're done sanding, diligently vacuum *everything*. You haven't come this far only to deal with unexpected particulate! After you vacuum the whole project, use denatured alcohol on a cleaning cloth to remove any remaining stickiness or sweat from the surface. Allow it to dry overnight. Now it's time to pour again. For the birch Kenai River countertop, I fell in love with everything a **self-leveling** formula has to offer. Using MakerPoxy meant that I had to do only one repair pour because it automatically settled into the removed sections and leveled across everything. Self-leveling products save a lot of time and money because you need to pour only one coat. The only difference between the two pictures below and on the next page is one pour. After removing more

than 2 gallons of uncured epoxy, the save-the-day moment came with a single repair pour that brought it all level again.

If you don't use a self-leveling formula, you may have to do multiple repair pours: fill the removed sections, sand the entire surface to level the epoxy, then pour a final topcoat for a flat finish.

Now that you know how to fix a major curing error, do you want to know why it happened in the first place? I didn't mix properly. When those two adorable puppies barged into the garage, I lost track of mixing time. When I went back to the mixture, I paused for a tingly little second, wondering, *Did I mix for five*

minutes? . . . Yeah, of course, I did! I poured the epoxy even though I wasn't totally sure. Lesson? Always err on the side of caution and mix longer it in doubt.

Invest in an old-fashioned, stand-alone kitchen timer, but don't forget that you can use any timer available to you: an oven, smartwatch, smartphone, voice-enabled home hubs, whatever works best for you. When mixing epoxy, I use what I fondly refer to as my mixtape, a flashback to my childhood. (If you didn't grow up in the 1980s or early '90s, it's a blank cassette tape recorded with a mix of songs.) When mixing, I may forget to start a timer or lose track of the minute hand, but I definitely know that three or four minutes have elapsed when a new song starts.

GET YOUR GRINDER

Here's a story that illustrates why you *always* should test a color prior to using it in a **large pour**. Jason Morena, the cameraman for Team GaryVee—a rad, high-energy group of people who work for Gary Vaynerchuk—asked me to make a table for the office in New York. I was stoked.

After carefully creating a design that I'd never tried before and spending weeks planning how to make it all come together, including shipping from Alaska, a light was shining at the end of the metaphorical tunnel. The table had just two **small pours** left and it was looking great, but it needed a little something extra to push it over the top. So of course I thought that would be a fantastic time to add a new color to the mix—that I didn't test first.

It looked like a symbiote from one of my favorite comic books had taken over the table. While the epoxy was transforming from a liquid to a solid (because science), it changed how the **pigment** reacted within the pour, result-

ing in a streaky, fluid mess. Worse yet, it didn't look wrong until *after* the table was almost done curing. By the time I spotted the problem, the epoxy had set almost to a **full cure**. With a problem like this, a drill or a razor isn't going to save your hide. You have to get creative and work around it—literally in this case because

I didn't want to ruin a layer of colored epoxy below the symbiote mess.

Sticky + **sandpaper** = mess, so I allowed the epoxy to cure completely. Then I busted out my **angle grinder**. With different discs, it ground away the cured epoxy in a controlled manner. It took almost 16 hours to fix and cost more money and stress than I can say. After grinding away all the symbiote epoxy, I used all the methods explained for the birch Kenai River countertop to clean up the rest of the job.

You're probably sick of hearing me say this, so I'll say it again. Keep your colorwork in the base layers. Because the colorwork ran low, the only difference between the two pictures on page 79 was a new pour of MakerPoxy. It filled the marks that the **angle grinder** had made and self-leveled across everything. Keep your complex layers low and your clear layers high, and you have a good chance to save your work if, no, *when* something goes wrong.

Recap

If you can't dig out the problem area while the epoxy is still pliable, let it cure fully.

- Use an angle grinder, rotary grinder (Dremel), or other device to remove unwanted sections.
- Clean the area thoroughly with denatured alcohol or epoxy cleaner and allow it to dry completely.
- If not using a self-leveling epoxy for the repair pour, relevel the project.
- Select the right epoxy for the repair pour. For example, you can't pour 2 inches with a coating epoxy. Mix the appropriate amount to fill the void.
- Allow the new epoxy to cure fully.
- If needed, apply a **flood coat** or topcoat.

WORST-CASE SCENARIOS

If you've done everything possible to save a project but it still looks beyond saving, step away from it for at least a week. In all my work and teaching, I have yet to see a botched project that couldn't be saved or transformed into something else.

One of my clients took delivery of a countertop but couldn't install it in the planned time frame. Because of how it was stored, the countertop turned into a moon bridge. It bowed so badly into a rainbow shape that they couldn't install it, despite a series of **kerf cuts**, bracing, and other out-of-the-box fixes. It was junk . . . or so I thought. I made them a new countertop and took the rainbow monstrosity back home. After some thought, it finally occurred to me that I could cut it into three smaller sections, work out the curve, and—*boom*—three coffee tables. By keeping an open mind and stepping away for a day, a week, or even a month, you can see any project with a fresh perspective. Here's how to reuse or reimagine projects that go off the rails.

Artwork

If the colors look wrong or other elements didn't work out as planned, peel the canvas from the wood and, using sharp shears, cut the canvas into random pieces. Use the pieces to make a mosaic, small inlays for jewelry (using UV resin), or sun catchers.

Countertops

If they're too damaged to repour or the colorwork has yellowed or never fully cured, sand them and paint them. Alternatively, you can remove the epoxy using the methods described earlier in this chapter. If part of a countertop becomes uncurable, saw off the sections that you can salvage. To repaint a countertop, lightly scuff it with an abrasive pad and apply **bonding primer** in the color of your choice. Then repour or repurpose it into a bench, desk, small tables, or wall art.

Pen blanks

Small items, including **pen blanks** and knife blanks, easily can turn into sections of new styles of pen blanks, knife blanks, rings, bracelets, or decorative inlays for furniture, for example. Use these small sections of cured epoxy to make **canes**, earrings, mosaics, bowl inlays, or other small items.

Tables

If a table didn't cure properly or had an accelerated **exothermic reaction**, repurpose the sections that did cure correctly into a coffee table, end tables, or serving trays. Salvage warped or uncured sections as outlined previously.

As you can see, you have lots of ways to repurpose a project that doesn't go as planned. But if the epoxy never cured at all, you need to clean the project and try to salvage the **substrate**. Clean the surface—wood, canvas, other—with epoxy remover or denatured alcohol and allow the substrate to dry. Sand or otherwise prep it again to give you a good base to start a new project.

IT'S GOING TO BE OK

OK, now it's time for you to start creating with epoxy. Move forward with one of the projects in the next section of this book or try your always-gloved hands at a project you've had in mind for a while. Some of my new students say, "I've had epoxy sitting on my shelf for five years, but I'm afraid to touch it!" But they leave the classroom with confidence. It can feel like a big step. You've made it this far. You're ready.

One of my favorite students was a man who makes jukeboxes. He'd been struggling to re-create the look of the multicolored lights that wrap around the devices, the "bubbler." He'd been trying to keep his colors from bleeding into one another. I was discussing a way to prevent that from happening, which you'll learn in the Lazy Susan project (page 131).

"Wait! I can do it that way?" he shouted to the whole class. "Why didn't I think of that?!"

Those fantastic teaching moments always remind me that we artists, builders, makers, and teachers still don't know so much about epoxy. Even I still don't know it all! I never want to stop learning, nor should you. My workshop has a whole bookshelf of notebooks filled with ideas about projects to try. The more you learn about how to manipulate epoxy into what you want, the more doors of possibility will open for you. The world of epoxy contains so much more than jewelry or river-style tables. It can encompass anything you want: a clear coat on a piece of wood gathered from a favorite hiking trail or camping trip, napkin rings, a holiday ornament, a display to honor your heritage, a commemoration of a loved one, a casement for wedding flowers, or 3D waves that remind you of your favorite beach. Embrace your imagination and release your creativity from the fear of using epoxy. Remember, build more than furniture. Build more confidence, build more skills, build more memories.

PART FOUR

PROJECTS

CHECKLISTS

All the projects that follow require some of the same steps to complete. You need to wear all the same **PPE** properly for the safe completion of all projects. Review basic steps and safety features before proceeding. Some projects require a deeper understanding of PPE and safety, which we'll address as appropriate. Different projects require different supplies and tools, but the lists below gather everything in one spot for comprehensive checklist purposes.

SAFETY REQUIREMENTS

1. No animals or small children allowed in your workspace.
2. Wear all PPE properly at all times.
3. Confirm proper ventilation or airflow in your workspace.
4. Confirm stable temperature of workspace.
5. Place protective coverings on all surfaces that epoxy may contact.
6. Elevate the project on a level surface and confirm level.

PPE

- [ ] apron: treated leather apron or thick, waxed canvas button duck
- [ ] eye-flush kit
- [ ] eyewash station
- [ ] footwear: plastic with no holes (epoxy only), steel-toed or carbon fiber (heavy machinery)
- [ ] gloves: disposable latex, nitrile, or vinyl
- [ ] goggles
- [ ] respirator

TOOLS

- [ ] **angle grinder** to handle errors
- [ ] brushes
- [ ] calculator
- [ ] **chip brush**
- [ ] clamps
- [ ] CNC or jigsaw
- [ ] **deburring tool**
- [ ] digital scale
- [ ] drill
- [ ] hair ties (if necessary)
- [ ] **heat gun**
- [ ] **torch**
- [ ] heating pad to warm epoxy
- [ ] level
- [ ] measuring spoons
- [ ] pliers
- [ ] room thermometer with humidity reader
- [ ] rotary grinder (Dremel)
- [ ] router
- [ ] sander
- [ ] scissors
- [ ] timer
- [ ] tweezers
- [ ] **UV light bar** if using UV resin
- [ ] shop vacuum
- [ ] saw: table, track, band

SUPPLIES

- [ ] alcohol: denatured for cleaning tools or epoxy errors and 99.9 percent isopropyl for spritzing on projects
- [ ] **bonding primer**
- [ ] cleaning cloths
- [ ] colorants: alcohol inks, dispersion **pigments**, **liquid pigments**, **mica powders**, acrylic paint
- [ ] epoxy
- [ ] epoxy cleaner
- [ ] epoxy remover
- [ ] finishing compound or polish: **flood coat**, oil (mineral, tung, linseed, walnut), shellac, wax (bees, carnauba), UV-protectant varnish
- [ ] glue: CA glue or wood glue
- [ ] hardener
- [ ] **liquid latex**
- [ ] **MDF**
- [ ] mixing cups
- [ ] mixing sticks: silicone or wooden (tongue depressors)
- [ ] **molds**: silicone or plastic (**UHMW** or **HDPE**)
- [ ] notebook
- [ ] paper towels
- [ ] plastic sheeting
- [ ] plastic wrap
- [ ] razor blade or craft knife
- [ ] cups to create tents
- [ ] **sandpaper** (various grits)
- [ ] soap
- [ ] spray-paint booth (collapsible)
- [ ] tape: **painter's**, **tuck**
- [ ] totes: rubber or plastic
- [ ] trash bags: heavy duty
- [ ] wet wipes
- [ ] wood sealant
- [ ] writing implement: pen or sharpened pencil

The Book Bookmark

BOOKMARK

This quick, engaging project offers a great way to dip your toes (not literally) into epoxy. This version calls for UV resin, but you can adapt it to use leftover epoxy from another project. You just as easily can use MakerPoxy, TableTop, **high-performance**, or even leftover thick-set epoxy. These bookmarks make great gifts, promotional items, or fundraisers.

Store-Bought Bookmark

SUPPLIES & TOOLS

silicone bookmark **mold** (page 204)

2-ounce cups (or smaller) for pouring

UV resin

mixing sticks

pigments (mica, liquid, or both)
in colors of choice

UV light apparatus or bar

deburring tool or 220-grit
sandpaper (optional)

tassel or string (optional)

1. Follow the Safety Requirements on page 84 and read all instructions before starting.

2. If your molds folded or otherwise look bent, allow them to settle in a warm room or in sunlight before pouring. They will re-create that shape when you pour because UV resin isn't heavy enough to force a mold into another shape.

3. Place the mold on a level surface.

4. Pour the desired amount of UV resin into a small mixing cup and use a clean stirring stick to add the color. Add only enough color to use within a few moments. UV resin starts curing as soon as UV light hits it, including sunlight. Mix completely.

5. Pour the colored epoxy into the mold. You can pour it in specific areas for a multicolored bookmark or the entire mold if using only one color.

6. Hold your UV light source over the project without touching the epoxy or slide the filled mold carefully under the light array.

7. Allow the project to "cook" for the time specified by the epoxy manufacturer.

8. For more than one color, add additional color and repeat steps 3 through 7 until you achieve the desired results.

TIP: It never hurts to give UV resin projects an extra pass under the UV light source to ensure that they cure properly and thoroughly. After demolding, consider using the UV light to add an extra cure to the back side of the project to catch any areas that might not have cooked completely.

9. Remove the project from the mold. Check carefully for sharp edges and scuff them lightly with sandpaper or a deburring tool to soften them.

10. If your mold has a hole intended for a tassel or string, attach it.

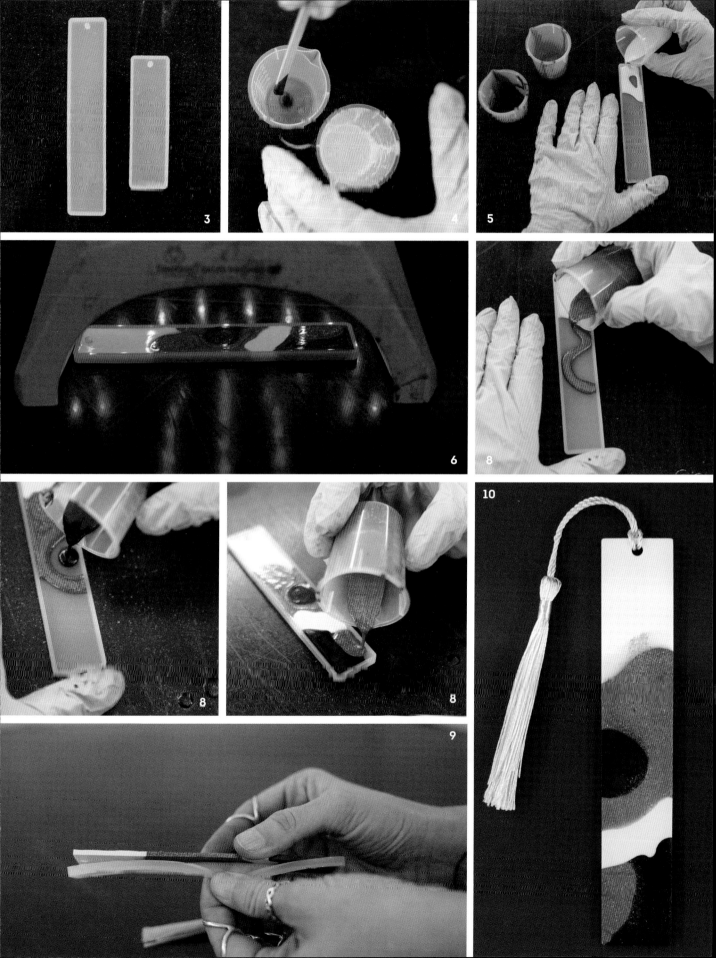

Handmade Bookmark

SUPPLIES & TOOLS

laser-cut (or otherwise cut) wooden bookmark (page 204)

small brush

wood stain or sealant of choice

220-grit sandpaper

painter's tape

2-ounce cups (or smaller) for pouring

UV resin

mixing sticks

pigments (mica, liquid, or both) in colors of choice

UV light source

tassel or string (optional)

1. Follow the Safety Requirements on page 84 and read all instructions before starting.

2. Using the brush, seal the wood with the sealant or stain of your choice and allow to dry overnight.

3. Once the stain or sealant has dried, lightly sand it with 220-grit sandpaper, if necessary, to remove any burrs or rough spots.

4. Affix painter's tape to cover the back side of the bookmark completely. Press *firmly* to eliminate any gaps between the bookmark and tape that might allow the resin to leak.

5. Place the bookmark on a level surface.

6. Pour the desired amount of UV resin into a small mixing cup and use a clean stirring stick to add the color. Add only enough color to use within a few moments. UV resin starts curing as soon as UV light hits it, including sunlight. Mix completely.

7. Pour the colored epoxy into the bookmark.

8. Hold your UV light source over the project without touching the epoxy or slide it carefully under the light array.

9. Allow the project to "cook" for the time specified by the epoxy manufacturer.

10. For more than one color, add additional color and repeat steps 5 through 9 until achieving the desired results. Work all single-color placements in the same pass. For example: all orange areas and cure, all black areas and cure, and so on.

11. Remove the tape from the back of the bookmark.

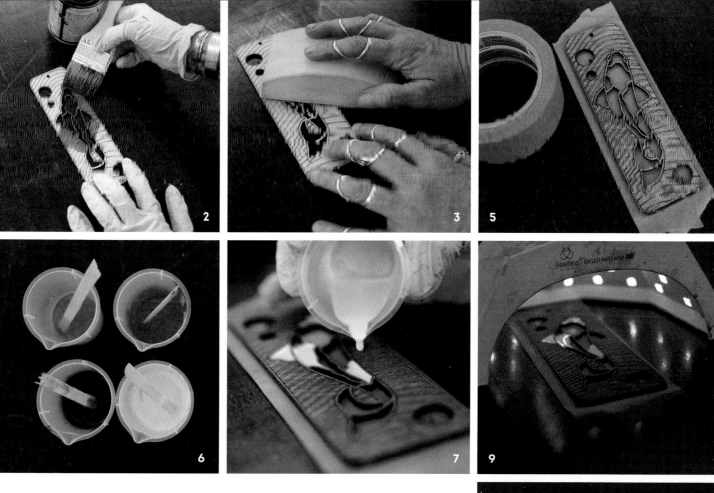

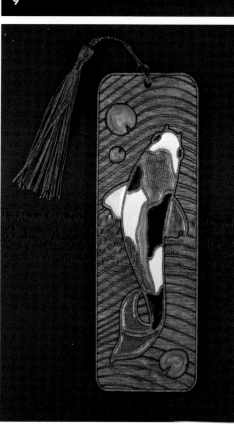

12. Attach a tassel or string if using.

Hey, look at that, you just completed your first project!

IDEAS FOR VARIATIONS

- Phone cases
- Small containers or trays
- Wall art
- "Stained glass" panels
- Sun catchers

Day-to-Night Coasters

COASTERS

Whether you laser-cut your own or purchase ready-made versions, coasters are always a hit and make great gifts. These coasters use just a little MakerPoxy, perfect for when you have a little left over from a bigger project. You can find the coaster file at JessCrow.com/book-projects.

Store-Bought Coasters

SUPPLIES & TOOLS

paintbrush

acrylic paint

coasters (page 204)

MakerPoxy

mixing sticks

round foam brush (optional)

acrylic markers, white and black

sandpaper (optional)

1. Follow the Safety Requirements on page 84 and read all instructions before starting.

2. Using a clean paintbrush and acrylic paint, paint the base of the coasters. If you're creating a day and night version, make the base layers a "day" color and "night" color. Allow to dry.

3. Mix only enough epoxy and hardener to skim the bottom of your coasters. The amount will vary based on the size of the coasters.

> **TIP:** If you're working on a nonporous substrate, you can measure the exact volume of epoxy that you need with water. But make sure to remove all the water and allow the coaster to dry *completely* before pouring the epoxy. Also consider using the epoxy calculator at JessCrow.com/epoxy-calculator.

4. Using a paintbrush or round foam brush, paint the sun and moon in the desired locations. Remember for accuracy that the sun rises in the east and sets in the west.

5. Using acrylic markers, add a small bird or other daytime details to the day coaster and stars or other nighttime details to the night coasters. You can add more items in the following steps. Allow to dry.

6. Mix enough epoxy to skim-coat the bottom of your coasters. Cure for 4 to 5 hours.

7. Using a paintbrush, add mountains, more birds, and more stars to the coasters.

8. Mix more epoxy for a final coat to seal the coasters. Cure for 4 to 5 hours.

9. If your coasters have a lip and you need to remove any paint or epoxy that has spilled over the lips, use 120-grit sandpaper to clean the edges.

10. If you've sanded the edges, use a small brush to stain the sanded edges and allow to dry.

Handmade Coasters

SUPPLIES & TOOLS

coaster file (page 204)

$1/8$-inch plywood

paintbrush

acrylic paint

round foam brush (optional)

wood glue or **CA glue**

MakerPoxy

mixing sticks

heat torch

acrylic markers, white and black

sandpaper or sander

wood sealant (optional)

1. Follow the Safety Requirements on page 84 and read all instructions before starting.

2. Using the laser file, cut the $1/8$-inch plywood. Don't assemble the coasters yet.

3. Using a clean brush and acrylic paint, paint the base of the coasters. If you're creating day and night versions, make the base layers a day color and a night color. Allow to dry.

4. Using a paintbrush or round foam brush, paint the sun and moon. Remember for accuracy that the sun rises in the east and sets in the west, which I forgot in this example! Paint the mountains as well and allow to dry.

5. Assemble the coasters in this order: base, celestial bodies, and mountains using the wood glue or CA glue. Apply glue around all edges to prevent epoxy leaks.

6. With mixing sticks, mix enough epoxy to skim-coat the bottom of the coasters and pour.

7. Use a torch to pop any bubbles.

8. Cure for 4 to 5 hours.

9. Using acrylic markers, add one or two birds and some stars to the cured epoxy. You can add more items in the following steps. Allow to dry.

10. For your final pour, make sure your coasters are level and pour enough epoxy to reach the tops of the coasters. You can stop at the edge of the mountains for a wood-and-epoxy look or pour over the mountains for a full-gloss finish. Cure for 8 to 12 hours.

11. Once your coasters have cured fully, lightly sand any drips on the outside edges.

12. Seal the wood with a foam brush or leave it raw.

IDEAS FOR VARIATIONS
- Earrings
- Phone cases
- Lazy Susans
- Circular trays
- End tables
- Wall art
- Bistro tables
- Coffee tables

CONTINUES

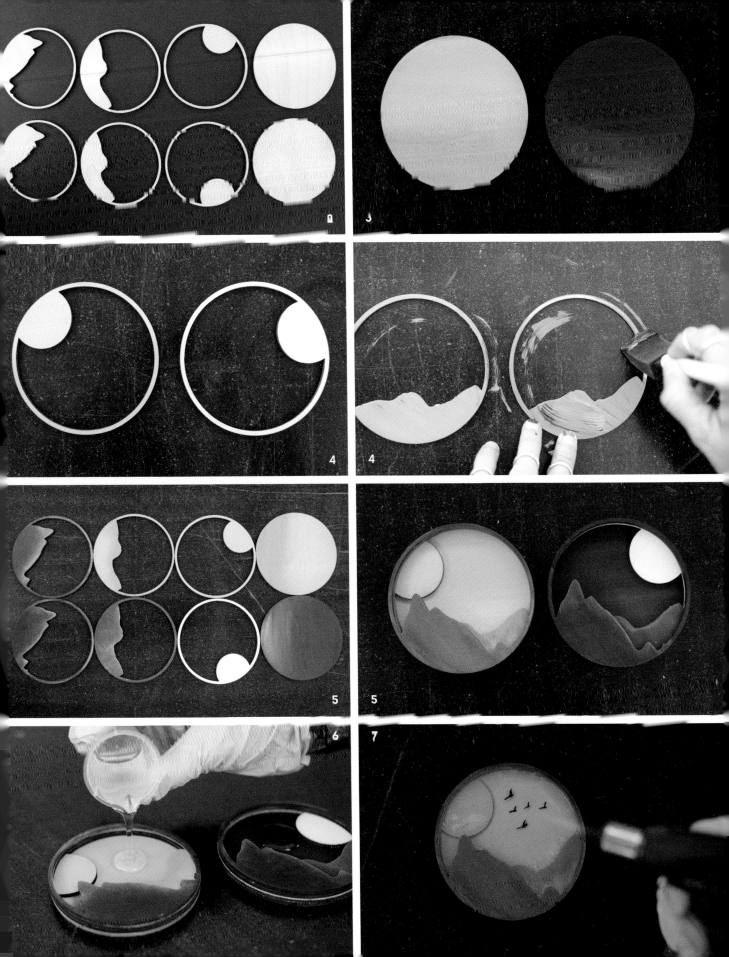

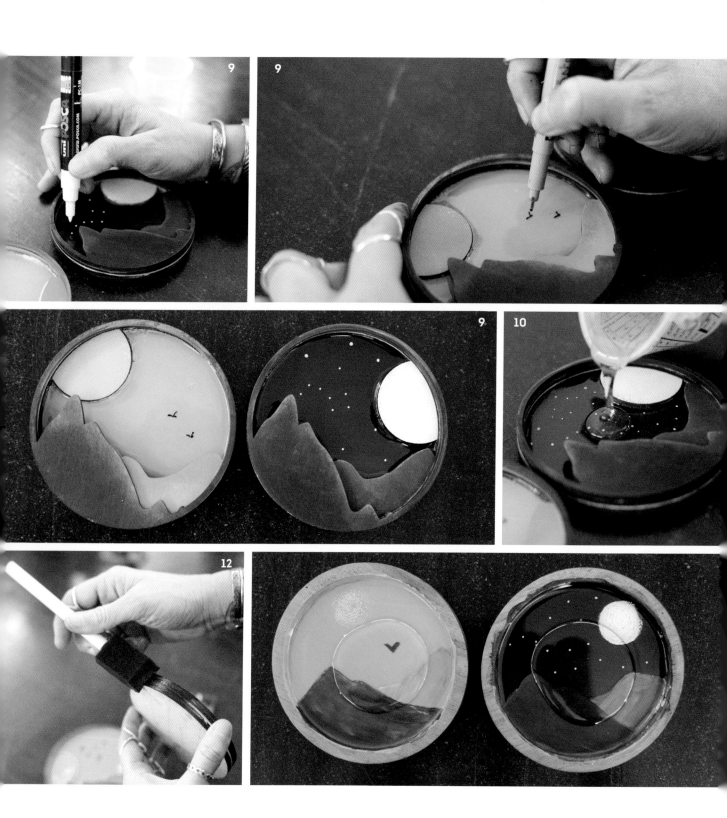

WAVE WALL ART

If you can't stop reminiscing about a special beach vacation, capturing the beauty of those waves will reconnect you to the water. For this project, you need a **1:1 formula** such as MakerPoxy or TableTop. The thicker viscosity of these epoxies helps with **lacing** and other effects that achieve a foaming-wave look. The colorwork boils down to personal preference. Deep, dark blues add depth, so I use more of those shades. If you prefer a brighter vibe and lighter colors, adjust the amount of pigment you add to your cup of epoxy according to your preference.

Ocean Wave Surfboard
Wall Art

Store-Bought Wave Wall Art

SUPPLIES & TOOLS

decorative surfboard (page 204)

painter's tape

cups or other leveling aids

level

5 mixing cups

mixing sticks

MakerPoxy or other 1:1 epoxy and hardener

mica powder, 3 shades of blue (page 202)

MIXOL liquid dispersion **pigment**, blue and white (page 202)

heat gun

fine-spray bottle

99.9% isopropyl alcohol

120-grit **sandpaper**

finishing oil or stain (optional)

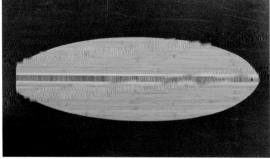

1. Follow the Safety Requirements on page 04 and read all instructions before starting.

2. Tape the underside of the surfboard to protect it from drips.

3. Place small cups or another means of elevation on a flat surface. Position the surfboard securely on the cups. Use a level to ensure the board lies flat and even.

4. Using the epoxy calculator at JessCrow .com/epoxy-calculator, measure the appropriate amount of epoxy and mix together parts **A** and **B** for 4 to 5 minutes.

5. Once you've mixed the epoxy completely, divide it among 5 mixing cups, one for each color of this project:

   - light blue (A),
   - blue (B),
   - dark blue (C),
   - white (D),
   - and clear (E). You need only a small amount of clear and white epoxy.

TIP: Leave a little extra epoxy in your main mixing cup in case you need or decide to add more of a color or don't have enough white.

6. Using a clean mixing stick, add the darkest blue mica powder to cup C, along with 1 or 2 drops of the liquid blue pigment.

7. Add your middle blue mica powder color to cup B. You can add 1 drop of liquid blue pigment to the cup, if you like.

CONTINUES

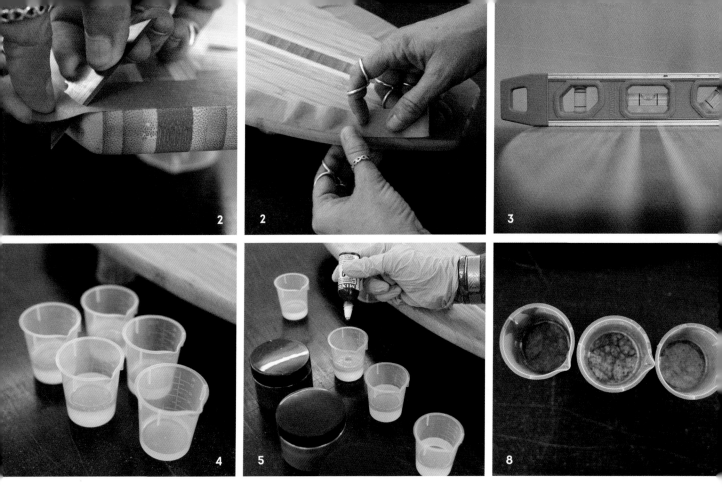

8. Add the lightest blue mica powder color to cup A.

> **TIP:** Here's a great trick to achieve a seamless blend of colors. Mix each color individually, as noted above. Pour a tiny amount of color A into B and mix. Repeat with a tiny amount of color B into C and mix. Don't add a lot, just enough to give a hint of the previous color. This technique ensures carryover of all colors, which will help with blending. Oceans, seas, lakes, and rivers often feature significant color changes with little or no blending, so this step is strictly optional, but it makes for an impressive effect in the final work.

9. After you've mixed the colors, stop to map your pour. Note how far up the board the blues should go and where you want the wave to break. Check your heat gun is plugged in and can reach all areas of your board. (If you're using the FURNO 300 heat gun, set it to maximum.)

10. Starting from the bottom of the board, approximately 1 inch from the edge, pour color C, the deepest color, in a wave shape.

> **NOTE:** Keep color C away from the edge because the epoxy will flatten and, when you add the other colors, you don't want it all to drip off the edge. That 1-inch buffer gives the pour room to level and keeps waste to a minimum.

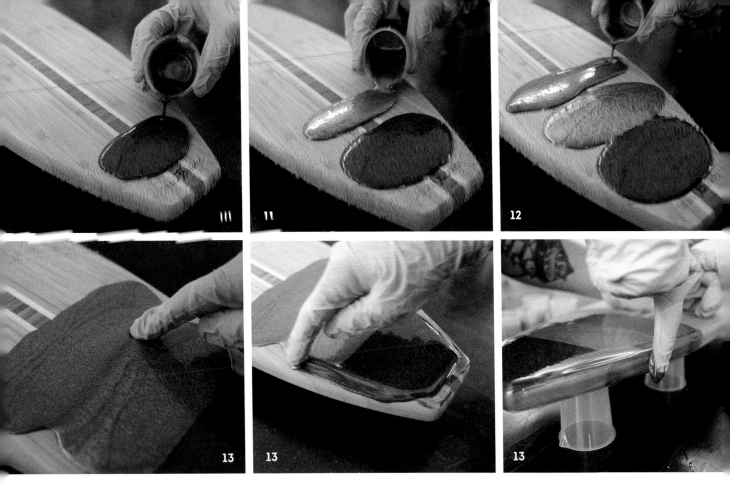

11. Pour color B ½ inch above color C. It's OK if the colors don't touch right now because you're going to manipulate them.

12. Repeat step 11 for color A.

13. Using a gloved finger, lightly blend the gaps between all the colors. No need to use a different finger for each gap, the colors will blend wonderfully; this step should take only a moment. You're closing the gaps, not trying to blend the colors.

14. Holding the heat gun 2 to 3 inches above the epoxy, make sweeping motions over it. This step just introduces uniform heat; the goal isn't to move the epoxy. It should start settling down, and the colors should start melding slowly.

TIP: Before moving to the next step, make sure your body dynamics feel under control. If you're standing in an uncomfortable position or if, while sweeping the heat gun over the epoxy, you had to contort your body, find a better position.

15. Holding the heat gun at approximately a 20-degree angle, feather color C into color B. Don't overdo it, though. It's better to go slowly and gently work the epoxy colors into each other rather than to **toast** the epoxy and end up with jelly.

CONTINUES

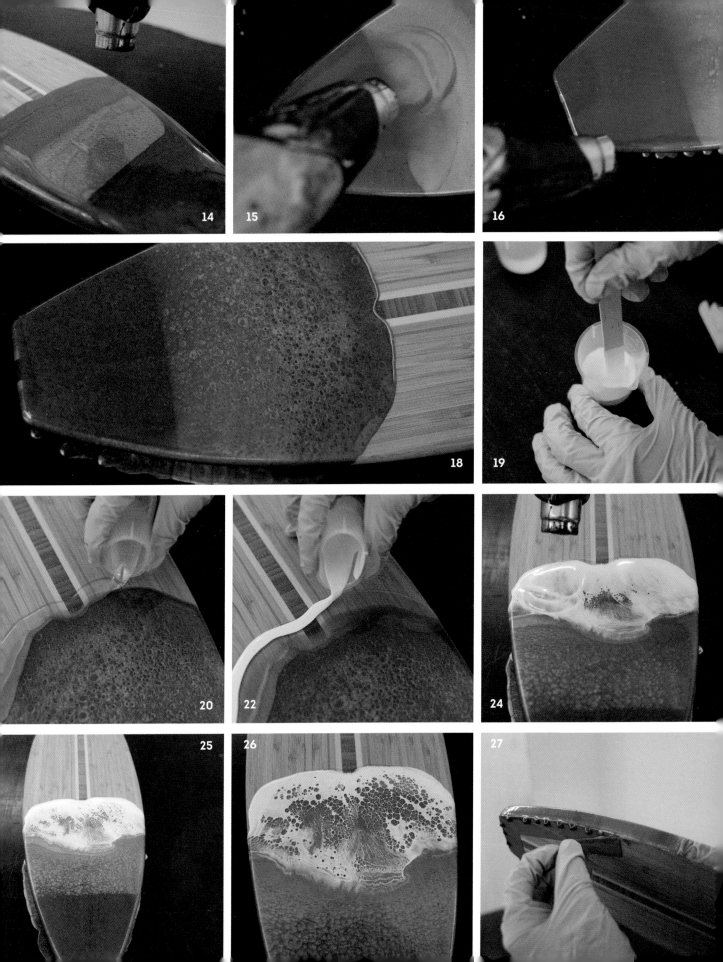

NOTE: At this step, either magic or frustration can happen. Approach the epoxy at an angle that encourages it to move but not burn. Work close to the project so you can manipulate the epoxy comfortably and easily see the colors blend. Hold the heat gun at a 15- to 35-degree angle to the epoxy. Change the angle as you move and blend. Sometimes 15 degrees will work nicely, whereas at other times a 35- or 40-degree angle may work better. David Sapp helpfully suggests that you hold it like a leaf blower. You want to push the epoxy from the base and flip it as if blowing leaves from the sidewalk. As you blend the epoxies, you'll see small ripples of color, a great indicator that you're holding the heat gun at the correct angle and moving the epoxy instead of burning it.

16. Repeat step 15 with colors B and A.

17. Pour the isopropyl alcohol into a fine-spray bottle.

18. Hold the bottom of the spray bottle 6 to 7 inches above your work and angle it slightly toward the ceiling. Spritz one time.

TIP: The alcohol causes the colors to separate, but in larger amounts it also breaks down epoxy. Don't spray so much that it creates dimples or bald spots. Just one spritz will bring a plethora of colors to the surface. More than that can cause the epoxy to separate from the wood. If that does happen, using a gloved finger, lightly tap the separation spot. The epoxy will close up.

19. Add a small amount of the liquid white pigment into mixing cup D and, using a clean mixing stick, slowly stir until it blends together fully.

TIP: When you've added and thoroughly mixed the appropriate amount of white pigment, you should see bubbles when you stop mixing. They look like carbonation bubbles, as in soda or pancake batter, not the bubbles produced by mixing. You always can add more white pigment to the epoxy to achieve the bubble effect, but exercise caution; it's a lot harder to take away white than to add it.

20. Gently pinch the mouth of mixing cup E, which contains the clear epoxy, and pour a line of clear epoxy across the top of color A that splits the difference. Splitting the difference means that half the clear epoxy should layer over color A and half should pour directly on the board, creating a thin line of clear epoxy across the top section of the wave that you completed in the previous steps.

21. Gently wave the heat gun over the clear epoxy. Again, you're not blending, just introducing heat to enable movement. This step should take no more than 4 to 5 seconds. Any more than that will start blending the clear epoxy into the blue, which you don't want.

22. Gently pinch the mouth of mixing cup D, which contains the white epoxy, and slowly pour it directly atop the clear epoxy that you poured in the previous step. Place the

CONTINUES

white atop and in the center of the clear epoxy so it doesn't end up on the board.

23. Holding the heat gun at a 20-degree angle, aim it at the top of the white section, the section closest to the board where there's no epoxy. Make a few passes to bring the epoxy to temperature.

24. Gently feather the white epoxy down the board. Don't worry about spreading all the white at one time. You can come back and move it down your board a little more.

25. Stop. Allow your board to rest for 1 to 3 minutes.

TIP: This step is always the hardest to learn. You need to stop feathering the white epoxy before it blends into the blues below it. The clear epoxy gives the white epoxy a buffer to float over the blue epoxy. But if you blend the white and clear too much, you'll end up with a light blue wave instead of a white one. Allowing the board to rest also allows you to see how the wave will spread and achieve the effect you want.

26. Aim the alcohol spray bottle toward the top of the wave and give it one more light misting. If you added the right amount of white pigment, as directed in step 19, the alcohol will cause an explosion of cells in the white epoxy, creating a dramatic foam effect. Again, don't overdo the alcohol; you don't want to create dimples or bald spots.

27. Once all the epoxy has cured fully, use your heat gun to heat the underside of the board. As you lightly heat the underside, pull the tape, which should release cleanly from the board.

28. Using 120-grit sandpaper, sand down any drips in areas where color has bled.

29. If needed, apply a finishing oil or stain to touch up the underside of the board.

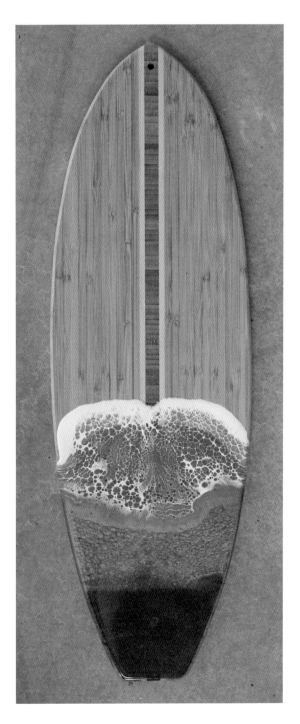

Handmade Wave Wall Art

If you're aiming for a particular feel or vibe, you can make this project from ½-inch or thicker plywood or any other wood. Surfboards come in a variety of sizes, from longboards to short boards. Making your own allows you to customize the piece to suit your preferences.

SUPPLIES & TOOLS

½-inch sheet of plywood or other wood

pencil

surfboard template

jigsaw, band saw, or router

round-over router bit (optional)

sandpaper, 60 to 220 grit

sander

1. Follow the Safety Requirements on page 84 and read all instructions before starting.

2. Using a pencil, trace your template onto the wood.

3. Following all manufacturer safety measures, use a jigsaw, band saw, or router to follow your pattern and cut the surfboard from the wood.

4. OPTIONAL: Use a ¼-inch round-over router bit to soften the edges of the surfboard. This step will allow the epoxy to flow smoothly, carrying the wave gently over the sides of the board instead of coming to an abrupt stop.

CONTINUES

5. Working your way through the grits, sand the top and bottom edges of the surfboard until you achieve the desired smoothness.

NOTE: Don't stain the wood now. If you do, the epoxy might not adhere fully to the wood. It's always better to stain projects with exposed wood *after* the pour. You can use a damp rag to wipe off any excess wood stain on cured epoxy.

6. Proceed to step 2 of the store-bought version of the project on page 101.

IDEAS FOR VARIATIONS

- Coasters
- Bowl bases
- Desks
- Tables
- Counters
- Floors

PROJECT

4

WALL CLOCK

In only a handful of places in the world can you view the spectacular aurora borealis, and Alaska is one of them. Taking inspiration from the winter skies, this clock will transport you to the Last Frontier in just one glance. The clarity and **doming** ability of MakerPoxy make the northern lights come to life in this window to the night sky.

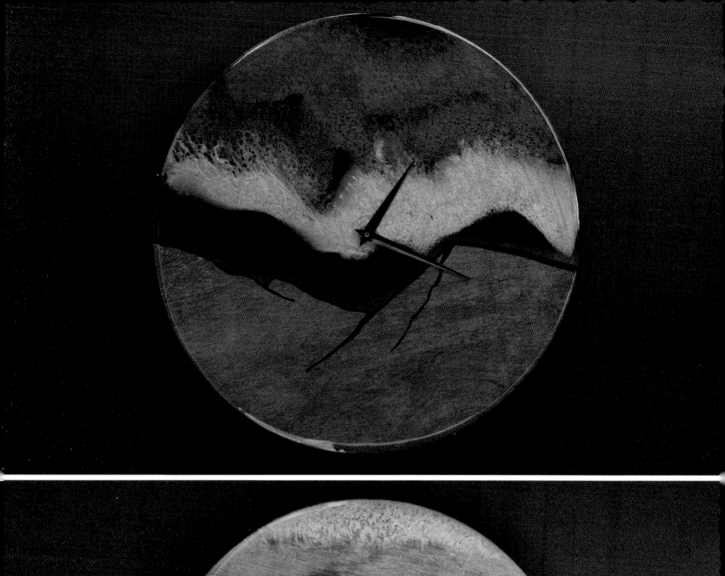

Aurora Borealis Wall Clock

Store-Bought Wall Clock

Rounds come in a variety of sizes, as do clock parts. Remember to scale the clock hands to the round. This project uses a 14-inch round.

SUPPLIES & TOOLS

brushes

alcohol inks: bright green, bright pink, and deep purple (page 204)

wooden clock round, unprimed (page 204)

MakerPoxy

foam brush

glitter-style **mica powder** (think stars) (page 204)

silicone spatulas (optional)

acrylic paint, black and white

stickers, vinyl cutouts, or more acrylic paints in colors of choice

sandpaper, 80 and 120 grit

wood stain (optional)

clock assembly (mechanism and hanging apparatus)

drill (optional)

1. Follow the Safety Requirements on page 84 and read all instructions before starting.

2. Using a small brush, paint a swath of the green alcohol ink on the top section of the round.

3. Follow the green with the pink and the purple, all on the top section. You'll tend to the bottom half in a later step. Allow the paints to dry.

4. Using the epoxy calculator at JessCrow.com/epoxy-calculator, measure the appropriate amount of epoxy and mix together **parts A** and **B**. For this step, you'll pour a layer of epoxy only $\frac{1}{16}$ to $\frac{1}{8}$ inch deep.

5. Mix just a little of the mica powder into the epoxy. You want the effect to appear faint to allow the aurora to shine through.

6. Pour the epoxy onto the wooden round.

7. Use a gloved hand, silicone spatula, or tongue depressor to spread the epoxy around the entire round.

8. Cure for 5 to 8 hours.

9. Paint the lower third or half of the round with black acrylic paint.

10. Use stickers, vinyl cutouts, or more acrylic paint to create a tree line. If painting, start at the top of the freshly painted black section and add lines for the tree trunk. Using the same brush, paint tree branches. Allow the paints to dry.

11. Using a white or light gray paint, add touches of snow to the branches. Allow to dry completely before moving to the next step.

CONTINUES

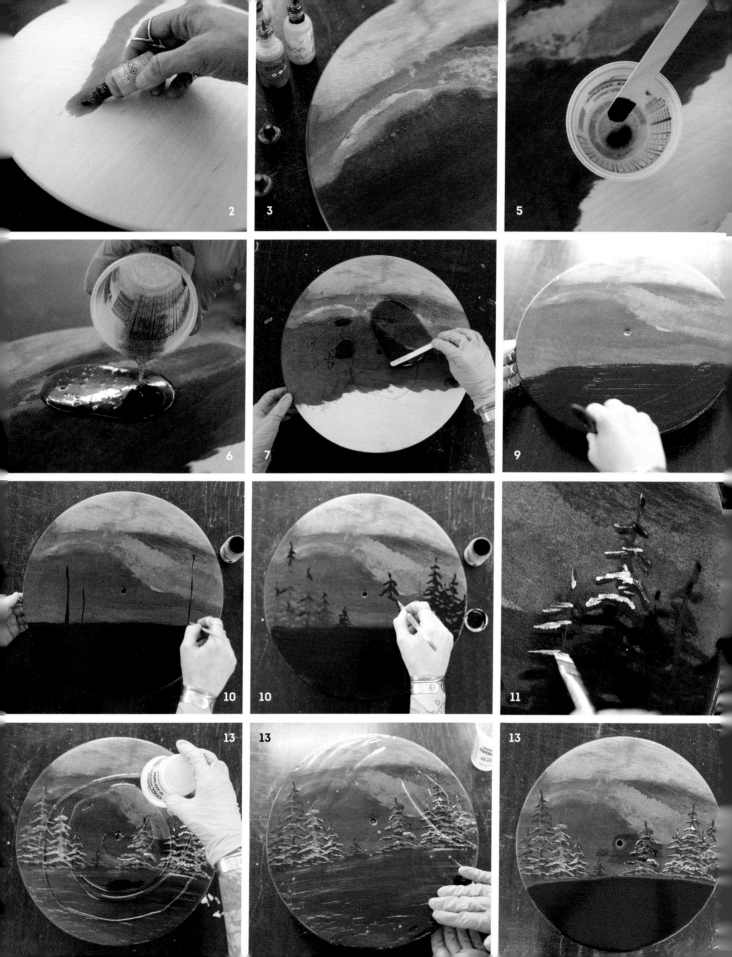

12. Mix another batch of MakerPoxy for a $\frac{1}{16}$- to $\frac{1}{8}$-inch pour.

13. Pour the clear batch of epoxy on the wooden round. Use a gloved hand or a clean silicone spatula to spread the epoxy around the entire round. Cure the clear epoxy for 8 to 12 hours.

14. Place the round face down on a soft surface.

15. With 80-grit sandpaper, sand down any epoxy drips that may have formed on the back. Follow with 120-grit sandpaper.

16. If needed or desired, stain the back of the wooden round.

17. Assemble the clock mechanism according to the manufacturer's directions.

TIP: If the central dial hole has clogged with epoxy, use a drill with the appropriate-sized bit to widen the hole.

For a slower, more controlled approach, roll a sheet of sandpaper into a tight tube and use it to sand down the epoxy blocking the mechanism from fitting in the dial hole.

18. Attach hanging hardware.

Handmade Wall Clock

Thinner plywood, 1/8 to 1/4 inch, works well for this project. Use a laser, **CNC**, or a router fitted with a circular cutting aid (as shown) to cut a circle from the wood.

SUPPLIES & TOOLS

1/8-inch or thicker plywood

laser cutter, CNC, or router with round jig (page 204)

drill or drill press

drill bit in corresponding size for the clock assembly

120-grit sandpaper

sander

1. Follow the Safety Requirements on page 84 and read all instructions before starting.

2. Determine the size of the clock you want to make. Using your laser, CNC, or router, cut the outside dimension of the clock face.

3. In the center of the round, drill a hole the size of the clock assembly.

4. With 120-grit sandpaper, sand any rough spots.

5. Proceed to step 2 of the store-bought version of the project on page 111.

IDEAS FOR VARIATIONS
- Picture frames
- Corkboard backings
- Heraldic coats of arms
- Mirror frames
- Sun and moon wall art

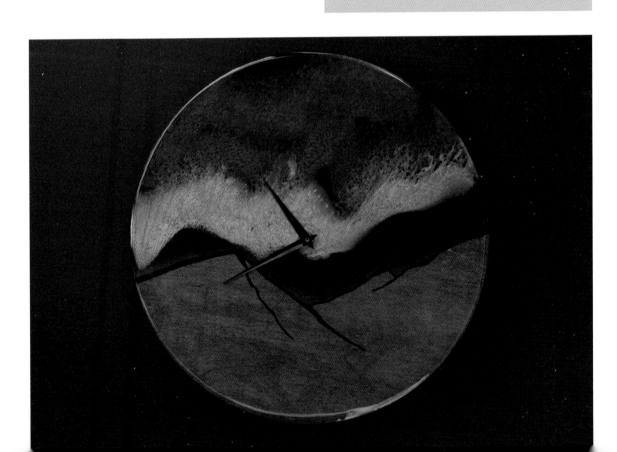

Variation

Between steps 3 and 4 of the instructions for the store-bought version, experiment with using tape to create a mountaintop.

1. Tear off a strip of painter's tape and place it on the round in the desired shape.
2. Paint the negative space that the tape creates black.
3. Pour brightly colored epoxy onto the round in an aurora pattern.
4. Using a heat gun and the 20-degree angle that you used for the Wave Wall Art (page 99), push the epoxy toward the top of the round.
5. Once the epoxy has set partially, which will depend on your environment, remove the tape and resume at step 10 of the instructions for the store-bought version (page 111).

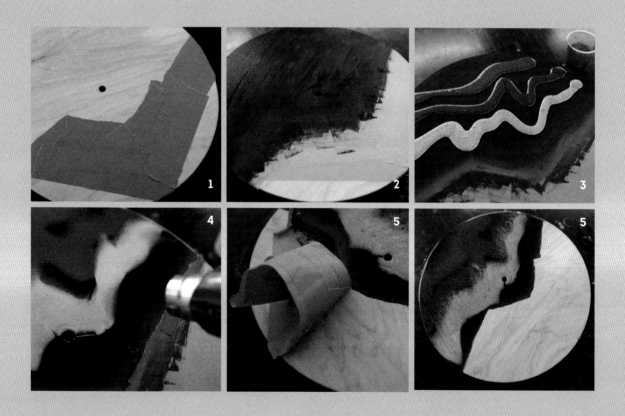

Store-Bought Kitchen Knife

Handmade Kitchen Knife

PROJECT
5

KITCHEN KNIFE

The handle design of this kitchen knife recalls the shimmer you might see in the sky, flying high above the clouds. Once you feel comfortable creating these knives, add names, flowers, or other unique details that bring meaning and joy to the recipient.

A **pressure pot** can help pull bubbles from the epoxy that might interfere with the small pins that hold the knife together. Bubbles in those areas can make it challenging to attach the scales to the **tang** or the back portion of the blade that connects to the knife handle.

The store-bought version of this project uses UV resin, but the handmade version uses ThickSet. Instead of ThickSet, you can use MakerPoxy, High-Performance, or TableTop, depending on the depth of your **mold**.

Store-Bought Kitchen Knife

Sourced online, this knife proved perfect for adding UV resin without needing a mold or building out a knife handle. UV resin can help you avoid drips that happen with epoxy that takes longer to cure.

SUPPLIES & TOOLS

painter's tape

blank knife (page 204)

paper towel (optional)

60-grit **sandpaper** or abrasive scrubbing pad

paintbrushes

black acrylic paint

holographic paint (page 204)

holographic shrink-wrap film (page 204)

UV resin and curing light (page 203)

razor blade

pressure pot (optional)

1. Follow the Safety Requirements on page 84 and read all instructions before starting.

2. Apply a couple of layers of tape to the knife blade for protection. A layer of paper towel gives added protection.

3. With sandpaper or a scrubbing pad, lightly scuff the knife handle.

4. Using a paintbrush, paint the handle with the acrylic paint. Allow to dry.

5. With a clean paintbrush, paint a thin layer of the holographic paint on the handle. You can blot it with a paper towel for more depth or leave it as is. Allow to dry.

6. For the next steps, you'll be working on one side of the handle at a time, in its entirety, before flipping it and completing work on the other side. Cut a section of the shrink-wrap about 25 percent larger than the handle of the blade.

7. Crinkle the shrink-wrap to create creases and folds, then gently flatten it, retaining the crinkles.

8. With the paintbrush, apply a thin layer of UV resin to the handle of the knife and the surface of the shrink-wrap.

9. Press the resinated shrink-wrap onto the handle of the blade, pressing it down with your fingers.

10. To cure the resin, apply the curing light for the amount of time specified by the manufacturer.

11. Using a paintbrush, apply two or three thin layers of UV resin to the handle. Apply one layer and cure; another layer and cure. Repeat until you achieve the desired depth.

12. With a razor blade, carefully trim any excess material from the edges of the handle.

13. Using the sandpaper or scrubbing pad, gently sand down any edges that the razor blade didn't eliminate. Turn the knife over and repeat steps 6 through 13.

14. Wash the blade with soap and water to remove any tape or residue.

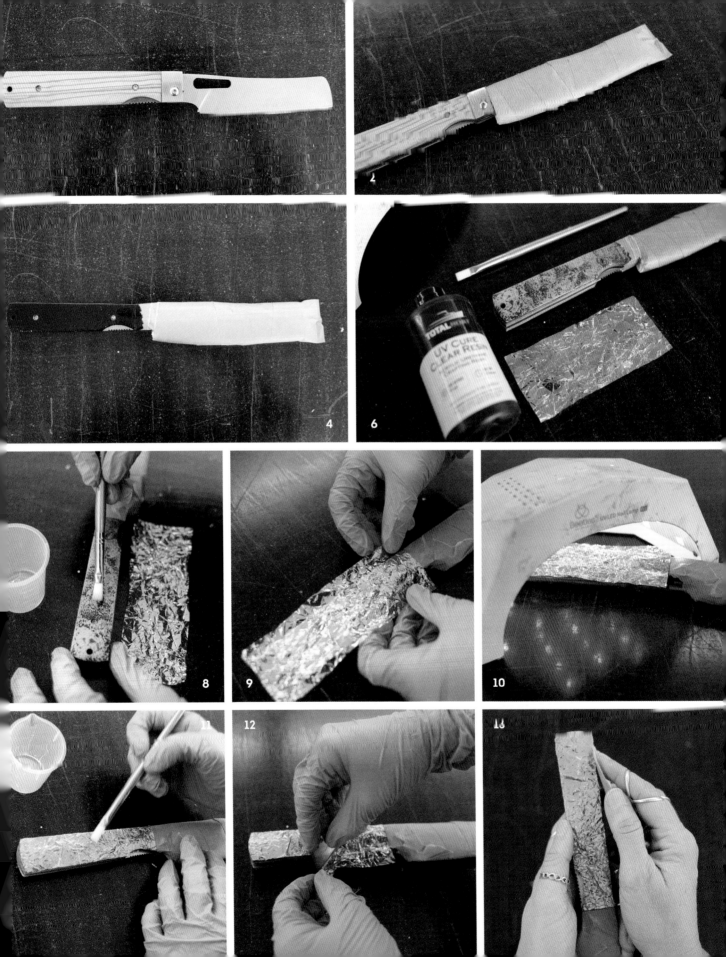

Handmade Kitchen Knife

Read any directions that come with your knife blank about how to assemble it. Altering the size of the mold for the tang can accommodate almost any blank for the following instructions. With molds, ThickSet, and a pressure pot, you can create depth and texture that will convince even the wickedest dragon to ask you for a new set of scales.

SUPPLIES & TOOLS

holographic shrink-wrap film (page 204)

ThickSet epoxy

scale mold (page 202)

mixing stick

alcohol ink in color of choice

pressure pot (optional)

60- to 120-grit sandpaper

painter's tape

marker or pencil

knife blank (page 204)

**drill or drill press with matching
   bit for the knife kit**

band saw or scroll saw

4-minute epoxy and hardener

small clamps

finishing oil (optional)

1. Follow the Safety Requirements on page 84 and read all instructions before starting.

2. Cut a section of the shrink-wrap 25 percent larger than your mold sections. Crinkle the shrink-wrap to create creases and folds, then gently flatten it, retaining the crinkles.

3. Mix the ThickSet epoxy and hardener.

4. Pour a small amount of epoxy into the bottom of the scale mold.

5. Using the remaining epoxy in your mixing cup, place the crinkled shrink-wrap into the cup to coat it. Remove from the cup.

6. Apply the shrink-wrap to the base of the mold. Use a gloved finger or a mixing stick to press the shrink-wrap into the mold, ensuring even contact with the bottom of the mold.

7. Pour the remainder of the epoxy into the scale mold.

8. Make sure the epoxy sits level with the top of the mold. If any of the shrink-wrap pokes above the surface, you'll have to sand it smooth when it comes time to attach the tang to the scales.

NOTE: If using a pressure pot, proceed to the next steps. If not, allow the epoxy to cure fully before moving to step 18.

CONTINUES

9. Place the mold carefully into the pressure pot.

10. Following the manufacturer's directions of the brand you're using, lock the lid and set the pressure. TotalBoat ThickSet, for example, recommends 50 PSI. *Don't exceed the maximum pressure rating of your pot.*

11. Allow to cure under pressure for 48 hours.

12. Carefully following the instructions for the pressure pot, release the pressure and remove the mold from the pot.

13. Remove the cured epoxy from the mold.

14. If any of the shrink-wrap has risen above the edges of the mold, sand it flat before moving on to the next steps.

> **NOTE:** You have many ways to attach blanks to the tang of a knife. Some folks like to attach the blanks and then cut and sand down the edges, while others like to rough out the blanks on a band saw or scroll saw before attaching them. Either way, don't remove too much material around the edges of the knife or you might end up with an exposed tang. Consider doing a rough-draft cut before gluing an epoxy blank to the tang, then dial it in when attaching the blank to the tang. If this is your first time making a knife blank, closely follow the directions that came with the kit.

15. Wrap the tape around the knife blade to protect yourself from cuts.

16. Using a marker or pencil, outline the knife tang on the blank. If your kit came with a template, use that to trace the tang.

17. Using a drill or drill press, drill holes into the blank where the attachment pins go. Make sure the bit matches the size of the pins.

18. Test fit the pins and blank on the tang.

19. Once you've determined that the pins fit and your trace marks are correct, use the band saw or scroll saw to cut the rough draft of the tang.

20. Following the directions, mix a small amount of 4-minute epoxy and apply it to the underside of the blank. Don't let any epoxy get into sections of the knife that could interfere with closing the blade.

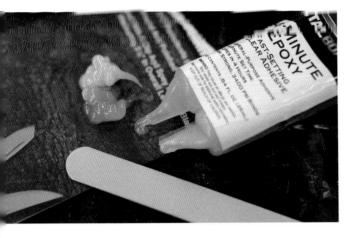

21. Attach the blank to the tang of the knife.

22. Set the pins in place. Clamp the knife and allow it to dry for a few minutes.

23. Repeat steps 20 through 24 on the other side of the knife.

24. Once the 4-minute epoxy has cured, fine tune the outline of the tang either by sanding it or trimming it on the band or scroll saw.

25. OPTIONAL: Use sandpaper to round over the edges of the epoxy to soften the handle grip.

26. OPTIONAL: Apply a finishing oil to the epoxy if you've sanded it and want a semi-gloss or glossy finish.

27. Wash the blade with soap and water to remove any tape or residue from it.

IDEAS FOR VARIATIONS
- Hair clips
- Bracelets
- Pocketknives
- Flat pens
- Garden tools
- Musical instrument inlays

Sunset Charcuterie Board

CHARCUTERIE BOARD

We all need to pause and watch the sun rise or set more often. Capturing that moment on a charcuterie board provides a special moment to remember and a reminder to slow down and take in the view. Both the store-bought and handmade versions of the board use vinyl cutouts, and well-chosen stickers can remove the fear of hand painting. MakerPoxy best suits this project, but any thick **1:1 formula** should work just as well.

Store-Bought Charcuterie Board

SUPPLIES & TOOLS

charcuterie board

painter's tape or 120-grit **sandpaper**

acrylic paints in colors of choice

foam brush

palm tree stickers or vinyl decals

320-grit sandpaper (optional)

acrylic marker, black

MakerPoxy

torch

finishing oil

1. Follow the Safety Requirements on page 84 and read all instructions before starting.

2. Tape the back side of your board. (If you prefer, you can sand it, using 120 grit, after you're done.)

3. With the handle facing up, place a length of tape approximately a third of the way down the board.

4. Place 4 dollops of acrylic paint in a vertical line on your board.

TIP: If you're struggling to decide which colors to use, watch the sunset or sunrise for ideas or search the Internet for images and match those colors at your local craft store or online.

5. Starting at the top, use the foam brush to spread the first color into a solid stripe across the handle of your board.

6. Using the same brush, paint the next color. Repeat for the two remaining colors, overlapping and blending them together. Allow to dry.

7. Place the stickers directly above the tape. Press down firmly to ensure maximum contact with the board.

TIP: If a sticker doesn't adhere properly, lightly sand the board with 320-grit sandpaper being cautious to not remove the paint from the previous step. Clean the board with a rag and use a new sticker. Press firmly to ensure that it sticks.

CONTINUES

8. With the acrylic marker, trace a line across the top edge of the tape, carrying the line to both sides of the board. Allow to dry.

9. Using the epoxy calculator at JessCrow.com/epoxy-calculator, measure the appropriate amount of epoxy and mix together **parts A** and **B**.

10. Spread the epoxy in a thin layer across the board, but don't pour a lot toward the tape line. The epoxy should touch the tape line but not go far over it.

11. Cure for 3 to 4 hours.

> **NOTE:** This intentionally isn't a long **cure time**. You want the epoxy to become stable but not cure 100 percent; otherwise, it might prove difficult to remove the tape.

12. Use a torch to pop any bubbles.

13. After three or four hours, check the tape. Peel back a small section of it to see whether the epoxy has set up and no longer is moving.

14. If the epoxy has set enough, remove the tape. You shouldn't need to heat the epoxy, but if necessary use your **heat gun** *very gently* to heat the epoxy and release the tape.

15. Allow the epoxy to finish curing completely, 8 to 12 more hours.

16. Use a finishing oil to finish the board. Allow to cure.

Handmade Charcuterie Board

For this version of the project, any species of wood will do. Select a flat board at least 9 by 15 inches.

SUPPLIES & TOOLS

½-inch-thick piece of wood

template (optional)

pencil

band saw or jigsaw

sander

sandpaper, 80, 120, and 220 grit

1. Follow the Safety Requirements on page 34 and read all instructions before starting.

2. Ensure that your board is flat and free of any defects. If not, address those issues with a sander and/or spot epoxy prior to starting your pour.

3. Either with the template or freehand, use the pencil to trace the shape of your charcuterie board.

4. Following all manufacturer safety measures, use a jigsaw or band saw to follow your pattern and cut the board.

5. From smallest grit to largest, sand all edges and the front and back of the board.

6. Proceed to step 2 of the store-bought version of the project on page 126.

IDEAS FOR VARIATIONS
- Bookmarks
- Notebook covers
- Picture frames
- Clocks
- Chair bases
- Wall art
- Desks
- Tables
- Counters

CONTINUES

LAZY SUSAN

If mist and mountains don't do it for you, other design options for this project include grassland, a seascape, an underwater vista, and much more. High-Performance epoxy or MakerPoxy best suits this project because you want something that will cure clear and allow the artwork to shine. If you're nervous about using paint, use stickers, magazine clippings, stamps, or anything else that strikes your fancy to achieve a comparable result.

Store-Bought Lazy Susan

SUPPLIES & TOOLS

lazy Susan (page 204)

painter's tape or 120-grit **sandpaper**

acrylic paints in black, gray, cream, dark green, and white

brushes

MakerPoxy or High-Performance

circular foam brush

heat gun

1. Follow the Safety Requirements on page 84 and read all instructions before starting.

2. Tape the bottom of the lazy Susan or leave it bare and plan to sand any epoxy drips at the end.

3. Prime the lazy Susan with black, gray, and cream acrylic paint. It may take multiple coats to achieve an opaque look, which will depend on the paints you've selected.

4. Mix enough MakerPoxy to brush a thin coat on the lazy Susan.

5. Cure for 3 to 5 hours.

6. Using dark green paint, add the first layer of the tree line to the lower third of the lazy Susan. Don't worry about creating perfect trees. They're standing in the distance, and mist will hide them partially. Allow to dry.

7. Using the foam brush, dab cream or white paint on the tree line for mist. Use a rag to blot any excess paint.

8. Carry the mist over the lazy Susan with the foam brush. On this first layer, think of mist as low-flying background clouds to help you visualize where to place it.

CONTINUES

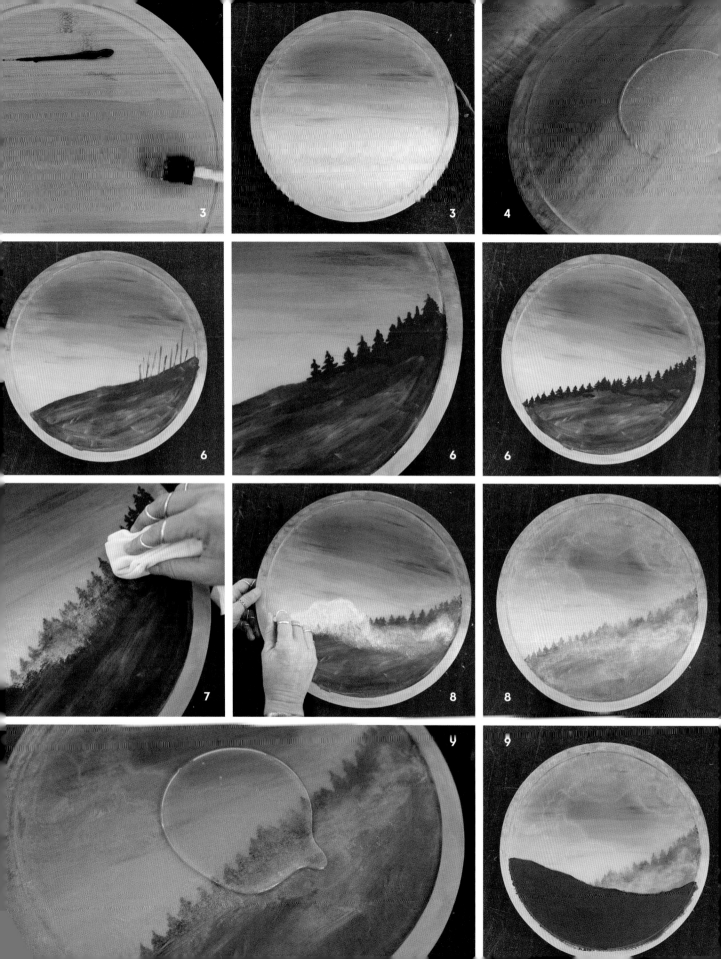

9. Repeat steps 4 through 7 two or three more times until you achieve the desired results.

> **TIP:** As you create the tree line, consistently work either left to right or right to left. Also remember that the closer the trees are to the sight line, the larger and more colorful they'll look. As you move through the layers, increase the size of your trees. Create a view as if standing on an adjacent mountain, watching the mist roll through the trees.

10. After pouring the last thin layer of epoxy in the tree line, paint the frame black or another color of choice. Allow to dry completely.

11. Mix enough MakerPoxy to cover the entire lazy Susan evenly, including the painted frame.

12. Use a gloved hand and a heat gun to distribute the epoxy evenly over the entire surface of the lazy Susan.

13. Cure for 8 to 12 hours.

14. Flip the lazy Susan over and, using 120-grit sandpaper, lightly sand down any small drips. Alternatively, gently use a heat gun to remove the painter's tape if applied.

IDEAS FOR VARIATIONS
- Earrings
- Rotating organizers for kitchen, bathroom, laundry, or crafting
- Circular trays
- End tables
- Wall art
- Bistro tables
- Coffee tables

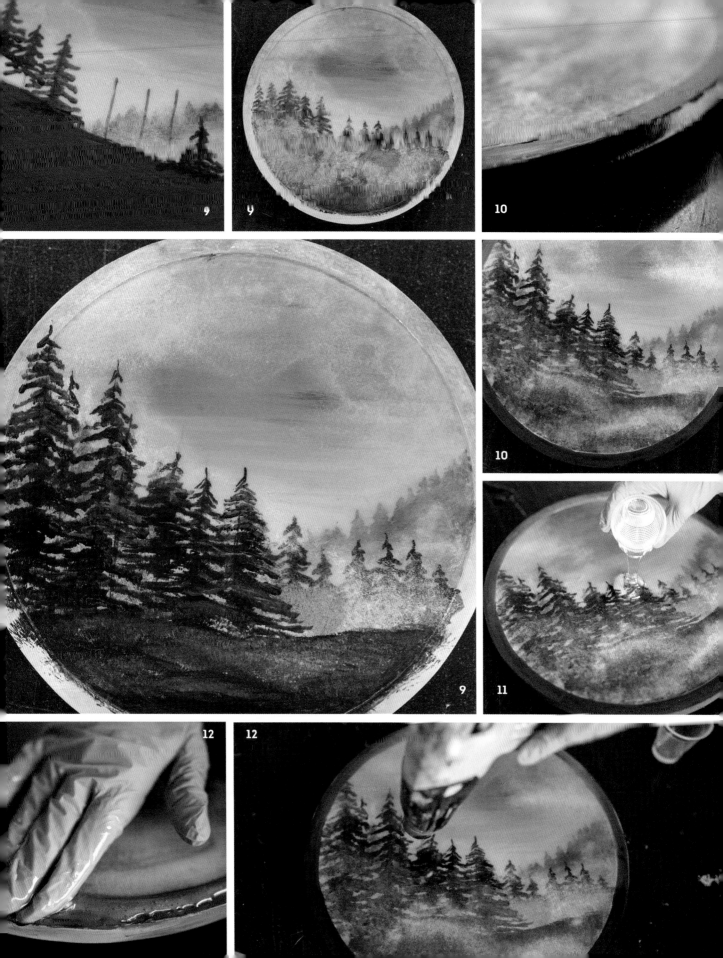

Through the Mist Lazy Susan

Handmade Lazy Susan

SUPPLIES & TOOLS

¼- to ½-inch-thick plywood

wood glue or **CA glue**

lazy Susan hardware (page 204)

laser, **CNC**, or router with
circle attachment

sander

sandpaper

1. Follow the Safety Requirements on page 84 and read all instructions before starting.

2. Using your laser, CNC, or router, cut a 14-inch disc from the plywood.

> **TIP:** If using ¼-inch plywood, cut two discs and glue them together, using wood glue or CA glue. On its own, ¼-inch wood will be slightly too thin for this project.

3. Lightly sand the plywood to remove any burrs or rough spots.

4. OPTIONAL: Create a lip for the lazy Susan by cutting another 14-inch disc from the plywood, then cut a 13-inch disc from the new 14-inch disc, resulting in a 13-inch disc (which you can use for another project) and a 14-inch ring. Glue the ring to the primary lazy Susan disc, using wood glue or CA glue, and allow it to dry before moving to the next step.

5. Attach the lazy Susan hardware to the plywood either with the small screws provided or CA glue. If gluing, allow the glue to dry completely before moving to the next step.

6. Proceed to step 2 of the store-bought version of the project on page 132.

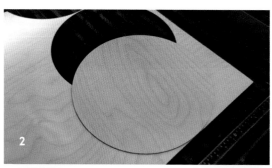

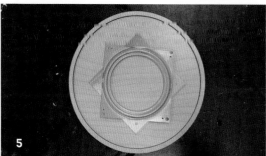

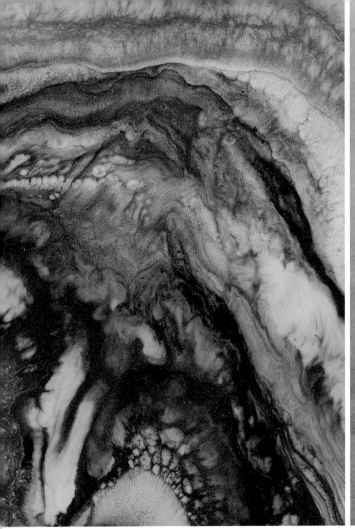

Magic Trip End Table

END TABLE

When I was developing this end table, which is one of my absolutely favorite projects, working on it filled my brain with nothing but thoughts of *I wonder . . .* and the astonishment of watching magic explode from just a few ingredients. In the photos, you'll see how laying down a pattern of pigmented epoxy offers endless possibilities for dramatic veining and dynamic movement that can make this table ideal for its intended space. Use MakerPoxy for this project. Don't substitute TableTop, which has a shorter working time—a huge drawback in this instance. If you need a refresher on selecting colors, see page 40.

Store-Bought End Table

SUPPLIES & TOOLS

small end table (page 204)

plastic sheeting (optional)

razor blade

sandpaper, 120 and 220 grit

white **bonding primer**

paintbrush

painter's tape

MakerPoxy

Black Diamond ghost gold **mica powder** (page 204)

alcohol inks in opposite/complementary colors (A and B) (page 204)

MIXOL **liquid pigments** in same colors as the alcohol inks or opposites

7 mixing cups

mixing sticks

fine-spray bottle filled with 99.9 percent isopropyl alcohol

heat gun

1. Follow the Safety Requirements on page 84 and read all instructions before starting.

2. If the table's legs are attached, remove them. If you can't remove them, use plastic sheeting and painter's tape to protect them.

3. Lightly scuff the top of the end table with 120-grit sandpaper.

4. Clean the surface of the table with a damp rag and allow it to dry.

5. Paint the top and sides of the table with the bonding primer. Allow it to dry. Repeat if any wood grain shows through the primer.

6. Lightly sand the top of the table with 220-grit sandpaper, smoothing the surface without removing the bonding primer.

7. Clean the table with a damp rag to remove all particulate and allow it to dry.

8. Tape the underside of the table and use a razor blade to slice off the overhanging tape.

9. Using the epoxy calculator at JessCrow .com/epoxy-calculator, measure the appropriate amount of epoxy. Set the thickness option to ¼ inch. This project will require drip-over, so you'll need more epoxy than usual to give the table surface the look of granite or quartz. Note below that you'll be using *more* than this amount to create colored epoxy, so make sure you have enough on hand.

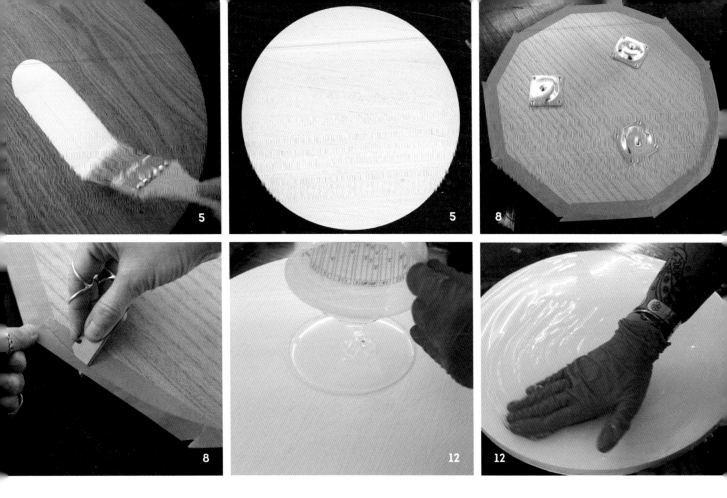

10. Remove the caps from all the alcohol inks. You'll be squirting them straight from the bottle, and it's difficult to remove caps with sticky gloves.

11. Pour the MakerPoxy into 7 cups as follows:
    - Cups 1–4: equal parts mixed epoxy. You'll tint these.
    - Cups 5–6: equal parts mixed epoxy, untinted. Set aside.
    - Cup 7: the amount you calculated in step 9. You need enough epoxy to coat the top of the table in a visibly dripping layer of MakerPoxy. If you run short, use some epoxy from cup 5 or 6.

12. Pour the MakerPoxy from cup 7 onto the center of the table's surface. Using a gloved hand, gently spread it around.

TIP: Use your hand, rather than a tool, in this step. If you use a scraper or mixing stick to spread the epoxy, you can't get a good sense of how deep the epoxy is and you run the risk of spreading it too thin. Keep extra gloves nearby so you can replace dirty ones easily.

13. Make the tinted epoxies in cups 1–4:
    - Cup 1: add an extra-large heap of ghost gold mica powder; the epoxy should resemble pourable honey.
    - Cup 2: add enough alcohol ink color A to tint the entire cup.
    - Cup 3: add enough alcohol ink color B to tint the entire cup.
    - Cup 4: add enough MIXOL liquid pigment to tint the entire cup of epoxy; it should look opaque.

CONTINUES

NOTE: You can achieve an explosive **lacing** pattern in the epoxy by starting your pour in the center of the tabletop and stacking tinted epoxies atop one another, a process that creates a complex **chemical reaction** between the epoxy, alcohol, and **pigments**. Remember when we discussed (page 19) how epoxy expands and then contracts when heated? Veining is a dramatic example of that phenomenon. In the photo below, you'll see what appears like a swath of blue epoxy lying next to brown, then yellowish epoxy, then brown epoxy again. But really it has a coating of gold epoxy poured directly atop it, separating the brown epoxy down the center. Keep this stacking technique in mind to achieve spectacular veining in your work.

Also, a heat gun is absolutely a must for this project. A **torch** won't work at all.

14. Pour the gold-tinted epoxy in a thin stripe across the middle of the tabletop.

15. Directly from the container, squirt a line of alcohol ink color A across the top of the gold stripe you poured in step 14. Repeat with alcohol ink color B. OPTIONAL: Aim your heat gun at the colorwork to help disperse the pigment into the epoxy.

16. Using cup 2, pour a stripe of epoxy directly atop the stripe that you poured in step 14. Aim your heat gun directly on the stripes that you poured in steps 14 and 16. Do two quick passes over the stripes. The epoxy shouldn't move much in this step.

17. Starting on the edge of the end table, use your heat gun to push the colored epoxy. Hold the heat gun at different angles. The epoxy will shift and change, depending on how much pigment you added to it. Aiming the heat gun directly atop the epoxy will create a blooming effect, while angling the heat gun at 30 degrees will push the color closest to the gun into the neighboring color. You're not trying to cover the entire surface of the table with these colors yet. Work in small sections, creating one small area of colorwork at a time.

TIP: Don't use the heat gun for more than 5 to 10 seconds at a time. Allow the epoxy to expand and then contract. Remove the heat from the epoxy, watch what happens, then decide if you need a few more seconds of heat to blend the colors more.

18. Repeat steps 14 through 17 either above or below the first colored pour.

19. Pause for 30 to 60 seconds to allow the epoxy to settle.

20. Hold the bottom of the fine-spray bottle of isopropyl alcohol approximately 7 inches above the table and mist the surface *only once*. Watch and marvel as little cells of color explode in the epoxy. (Chemistry's rad!) *Don't mist again.*

21. Run a gloved hand around the edges of the table. Don't worry about messing up the epoxy. It will continue flowing over the edges, carrying the colors with it. You want to make sure the epoxy has a good base to flow over.

CONTINUES

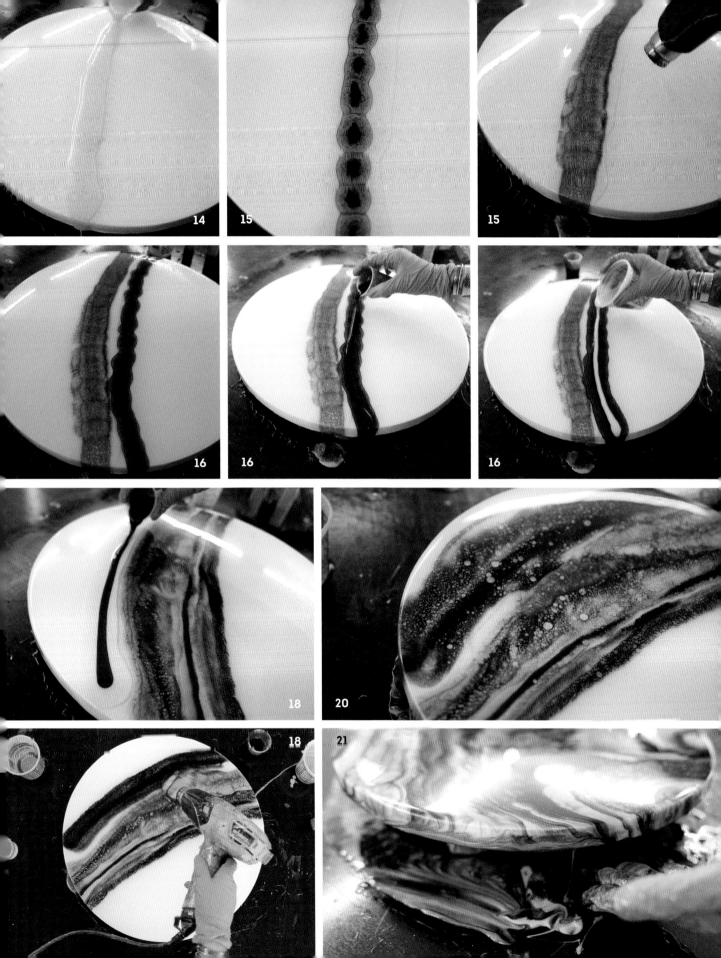

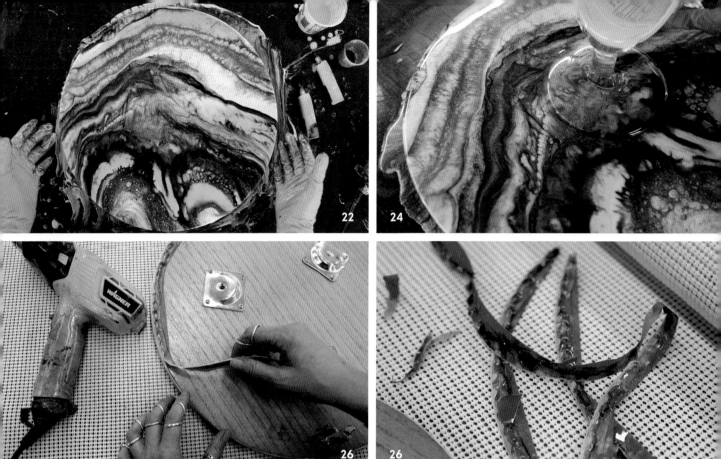

22. Repeat steps 14 through 22 until you almost have achieved the desired look. When you think, *I really like how this looks. I should do one more thing*, STOP. Due to the different weights of the components, the color will continue to shift for 5 to 15 minutes, depending on how long the previous steps took. Allow the color to settle before you make any more tweaks.

23. Cure for 8 to 12 hours.

24. OPTIONAL: Add a clear coat of Maker-Poxy for added depth and protection.

25. Cure the clear coat for 8 to 12 hours.

26. Flip the end table onto a soft surface and use a heat gun to remove the tape from the underside of the table.

27. Attach the legs.

Variations

Repeat steps 14 through 21 to cover the entire table. As you do, experiment with other colors and the following techniques to produce even more vivid, captivating results.

- Pour a thin stripe of alcohol ink color A directly on a section of the end table where you haven't placed any color. Pour a thin stripe of alcohol ink color B directly next to it. Pour a thin stripe of epoxy from cup 1 atop the alcohol ink and let it settle for 2 to 5 seconds. In a smooth motion, wave your heat gun over the stripe to warm the epoxy. Then come back at an angle and push the alcohol ink over the stripe from cup 1.

- Revisit an already colored and misted section of the table with a thin layer of epoxy from cup 1. Using a gloved finger or mixing stick, "draw" a line through the epoxy. Use the heat gun to soften the edges of the tinted epoxy.

- Pick up the table and lean it forward, backward, and to each side. The warmed epoxy will flow and the colors will transform.

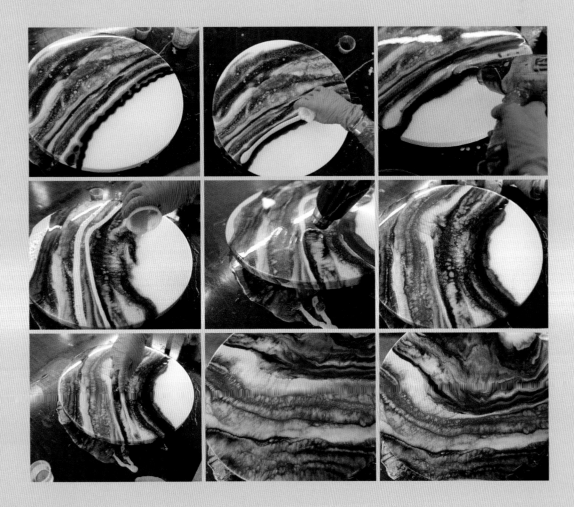

Handmade End Table

You're covering the entire surface of this table with primer and epoxy, so don't waste money on expensive wood. Hardware stores also carry unprimed wooden rounds in various sizes.

SUPPLIES & TOOLS

¾-inch or thicker plywood sheet

CNC or router with circle attachment

router

¼-inch cutting bit

$1/8$- to ¼-inch round-over bit for router

sander

sandpaper, 80, 120, 220 grits

3 or 4 legs, 16 to 19 inches tall

attachment hardware for legs

drill and bit that match the
   attachment hardware

tape measure

pencil

1. Follow the Safety Requirements on page 84 and read all instructions before starting.

2. Using the method you prefer, cut a disc at least 16 inches in diameter from the plywood.

3. Confirm *now* that the attachment hardware for the legs won't poke through the bottom of the plywood disc and ruin the build at the end of the project. If your wood isn't thick enough to accommodate the screws that came with your legs, use shorter screws.

4. Using the router fitted with the round-over bit, round the edges of the top of the table. Rounded edges ensure a clean pour over the edges. You can skip this step for a sharper, more modern, clean edge.

5. Starting with the lowest grit and working your way to the highest, sand the top, bottom, and sides of the table until no burrs (raised or rough edges) remain.

6. Proceed to steps 2 through 27 of the store-bought version of the project on page 140, then return here.

7. While the table is still upside down, use the tape measure and a pencil to plan where to attach the legs. To support the weight of the whole surface effectively, place them halfway between the center of the table and the outside edge. For maximum stability, place them as close to the outside edge of the table and as far apart from one another as possible. If using three legs, you'll create an equilateral triangle. If using four legs, you'll create a square.

8. Attach the legs.

IDEAS FOR VARIATIONS
- Coasters
- Clocks
- Decorative bowls
- Serving trays
- Desks
- Tables

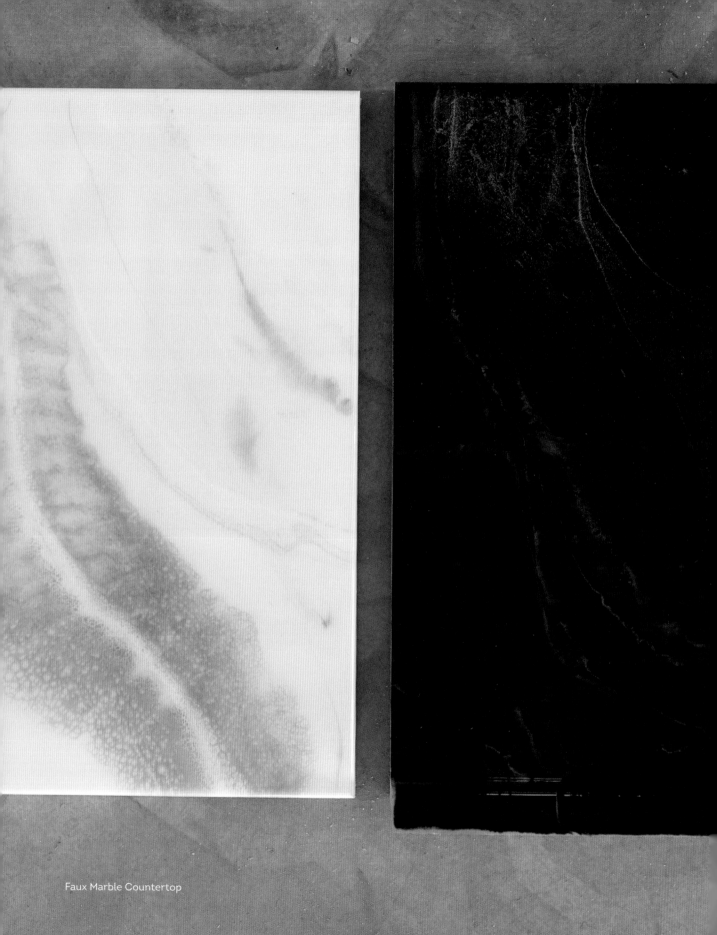

Faux Marble Countertop

PROJECT

9

COUNTERTOP

If you look at your kitchen countertops and wish you could redo them, this project is for you. Giving them a marble look requires more prep work than the pour itself. To give them more depth and durability, plan on more than one pour, as instructed in step 23.

Before you undertake the project, do a test pour on a 14-by-14-inch **substrate**. It will show you, in miniature, how the larger pour will look. You might not like the results, or you may love it so much that you want to double down on your design choices. Tests also establish a critical baseline for timing.

Choosing a **bonding primer** that matches the base color of your pour will save you money and time. If you're doing a white or cream-colored pour, select a white, cream, or gray primer. If you're doing a black or dark-colored pour, tint the primer gray or black, which will keep any areas that might not have received enough epoxy from poking through. This technique also adds dimension to the final project.

You absolutely need a **1:1** epoxy, such as MakerPoxy or TableTop. Its longer working time makes MakerPoxy the better option for color work and large projects. If you're doing smaller counters without a lot of color, Table-Top will work as well.

As written, this project ends with a glossy finish, but if you want a matte finish, which I prefer, check out the variation on page 155.

If you're doing more than one countertop at a time, plan ahead. If you're doing complex color-work that will carry across more than one surface, mix all your epoxy at once. You may want a vein of gold or gray to go across a countertop to give the appearance of a continuous slab of marble. If there's a sink or stovetop in the way, you need enough epoxy to get the job done but not so much that the volume will cause an accelerated **exothermic reaction** in the mixing container. If you have a kitchen island or multiple, noncontinuous countertops, mix and pour them as separate units.

Existing Countertop

plastic sheeting

painter's tape

sander, preferably with vacuum attachment

sandpaper, 60 and 80 grit (120, 220, 320, and 400 optional)

bonding primer

paint roller

paintbrushes

mixing containers and cups

mixing sticks

MakerPoxy or TableTop

colorant(s) in color(s) of choice

chip brush (optional)

heat gun

fine-spray bottle filled with 99.9% isopropyl alcohol

mica powder(s) in color(s) of choice (optional)

liquid pigment(s) in color(s) of choice (optional)

ventilation fans

CONTINUES

1. Follow the Safety Requirements on page 84 and read all instructions before starting.

2. Completely clear your work area, including any dishes or food. Yes, even the packaged stuff.

3. To protect your workspace from spilled epoxy, cover it with plastic sheeting, including the floor. Tape the sheeting in place.

4. Sand the countertop with 60-grit sandpaper. This step isn't removing the existing finish. It just roughs up the surface to allow the bonding primer to adhere.

5. Use a damp rag to remove any particulate from the countertop. Allow to dry completely.

6. Sand again with 80-grit sandpaper.

7. Use a damp rag, again, to clean up any residue or particulate.

8. With a paint roller or brush, apply the bonding primer to the clean, sanded surface. Cover the entire area where you plan to pour epoxy. Allow the primer to dry completely.

9. If the countertop needs a second coat of primer, apply it now. Allow the second coat to dry completely before moving to the next step.

10. OPTIONAL: The best way for allowing colored epoxy to flow smoothly is to roll or brush a thin layer of clear epoxy onto the primed countertop, then add the colored epoxy. Try this technique with a test pour and see if you like the effect.

11. Using the epoxy calculator at JessCrow.com/epoxy-calculator, measure the appropriate amount of epoxy and hardener. For larger batches, it's important to incorporate *all* the epoxy and hardener. To ensure thorough blending, mix the batches for the full time required by the manufacturer plus an additional 2 to 3 minutes.

12. Divide the epoxy into containers and tint according to your preference, fully mixing the colorant(s) into the epoxy.

13. If your countertop has a backsplash, pour a stripe of epoxy across the top. Use a chip brush or a gloved hand to spread it down the vertical section. It doesn't have to look perfect because you'll address this section last, when your epoxy is reaching the end of its **pot life** and will stick better to the vertical pane of the backsplash.

14. Apply the base color of epoxy to the countertop. Use a heat gun or brush to soften the edges of the pour or spread it around.

15. Add thin layers of epoxy. Consider color stacking (page 142) as well as a single **dirty pour** or a **side-by-side pour**.

16. Use the heat gun to blend the colors. Experiment with the angle of the heat to achieve different results.

17. To draw veins of color through the epoxy, use the tip of a mixing stick or drips from a paintbrush. These techniques can create a more delicate effect than pouring a thin stripe.

CONTINUES

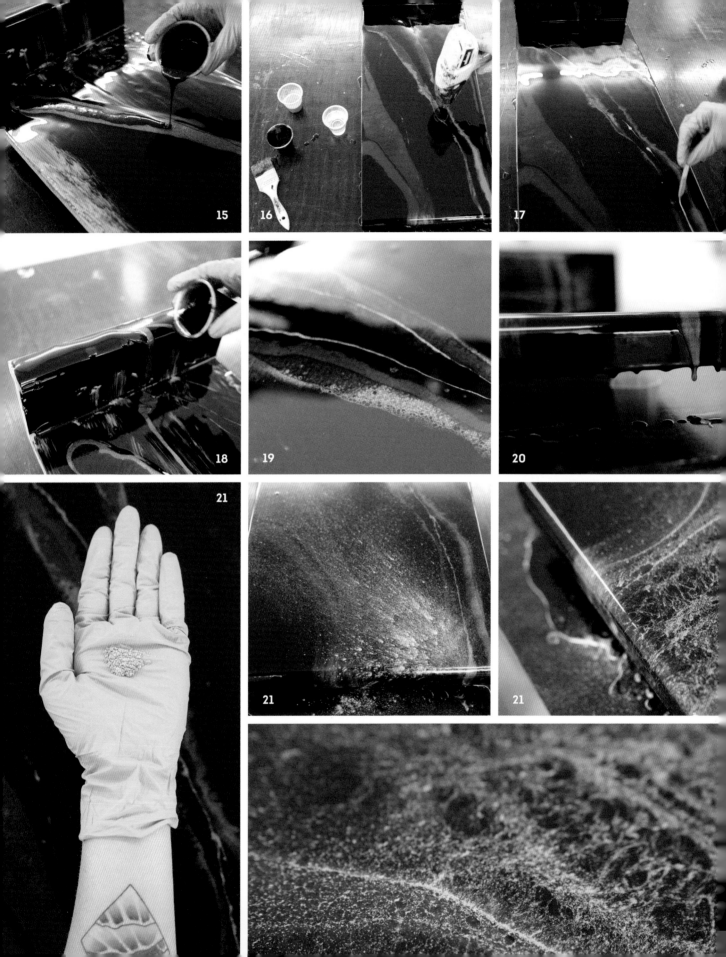

18. As you work the main, flat section(s) of the countertop, continuously apply epoxy to the backsplash, if present. The epoxy will continue draining down from the vertical pane of the backsplash onto the main section, creating a seamless transition.

19. Once you've put down a decent layer of base colors, use the fine-spray bottle of rubbing alcohol to mist the countertop. This technique, described on page 142, will give your work more dimension.

20. Occasionally run your gloved hand or a used brush over the edge of the countertop, making sure the epoxy flows freely over the edges and carries the colorwork down the sides.

21. OPTIONAL: Lightly dust mica powder onto the countertop. Allow it to settle for 60 seconds. Mist with the fine-spray bottle of rubbing alcohol. (This step will make a mess!)

22. Cure for 8 to 12 hours.

23. If adding another layer of color for depth, lightly scuff the existing pour with 80-grit sandpaper and repeat steps 11 through 22.

24. For a glossy finish, pour a layer of clear epoxy over the whole countertop or use a food-grade finish to seal and protect it.

Variation

For a matte finish, follow these steps. Change sandpaper sheets frequently to prevent swirls from forming.

1. Completely sand the countertop with 120-grit sandpaper.

2. Use a damp rag to clean up sanding residue or other particulate.

3. Repeat with 220-grit sandpaper and clean up.

4. Check for swirl marks that need attention. If an area requires further sanding, do so before moving on.

5. Continue the process, working into higher grits (up to 400), until you achieve the desired finish.

6. Apply a matte, food-grade finish to the countertop. Allow it to cure fully.

Handmade Countertop

SUPPLIES & TOOLS

plastic sheeting

painter's tape

tape measure

pencil

butcher paper (optional)

shop vacuum

1-inch-thick **MDF** or plywood

table saw, circular saw, or track saw

router

round-over router bit in
  appropriate size

drill and screws

1. Follow the Safety Requirements on page 84 and read all instructions before starting.

2. Completely clear your work area, including any dishes or food. Yes, even the packaged stuff.

3. To protect your workspace from spilled epoxy, cover it with plastic sheeting, including the floor. Tape the sheeting in place.

4. Accurately measure any existing countertop that you plan on replacing. If you have an odd-shaped countertop, make a template with butcher paper.

5. Carefully remove any existing countertop, paying attention to how and where it attached to cabinets and walls. If you've never done this before, take lots of photos. Label or add notes to each picture, detailing where and how the original countertops attached to the cabinets and walls. Refer to them as you build the new countertops.

6. Use a shop vac to clean all dust and particulate from the area.

7. Using a table saw or track saw, cut the MDF or plywood to the appropriate size for the new countertop.

CAUTION: MDF is *extremely* toxic if inhaled from cutting or sanding. Use your PPE properly.

8. If you're replacing a countertop that has a sink with an undermount, cut out the sink now. Use the router to add a slightly rounded edge to the top lip of the countertop. If you're replacing a countertop with an overmounted sink, you can cut out the sink before or after the pours. It's usually better to cut before pouring in case something goes wrong with the cut.

9. Using the router, round over the front edge of the countertop at the desired angle. It's important to add even just a little round-over to give them a nice edge. If you don't have a router, lightly sand the edge of the MDF or plywood to reduce the sharp, 90-degree factory angle.

10. Test fit the countertop *before* doing any epoxy work.

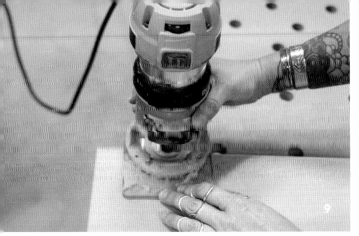

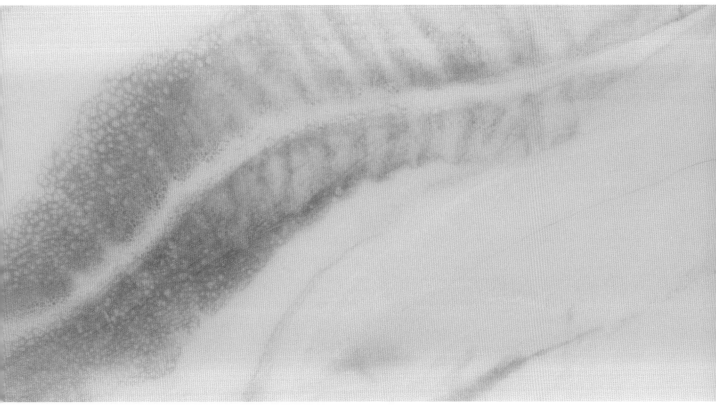

11. If using plywood, sand the countertop with 80-grit sandpaper to 120 grit to remove any burrs or splinters.

12. Proceed to steps 8 through 24 of the Existing version of the project on page 152, then return here.

13. After the countertop has cured fully, refer to your notes or photos and, with the drill and screws, attach it to the cabinets and walls in the same way that you removed it.

IDEAS FOR VARIATIONS
- Dresser tops
  Triptych wall art
- Desks
- Partitions

Riverbank Coffee Table

COFFEE TABLE

Creating a coffee table that captures the feeling of standing at a river's edge doesn't require a lot of artwork. You just need a few items from a nearby riverbank or store. Found items can help you re-create memories of a happy place—at home. If you're using natural items, such as sticks or rocks, for this table, make sure they're completely dry before placing them in the epoxy. Seal any porous items with clear shellac or a small batch of Maker-Poxy. You don't want them to create bubbles or an accelerated **exothermic reaction** in the table.

For this project, you need to use a **mold** or create one. (The steps remain the same for either approach.) In the photos below, you'll note that I'm using a store-bought mold, but you can make one (as mentioned on page 41) with **HDPE**, which you can use again, or with **melamine** (¾ to 1 inch), caulk, and silicone. Use water to test any mold for leaks *before* pouring epoxy into it. It's a lot easier to clean up spilled water than epoxy that's starting to set.

When finished, the table will run 2 to 3 inches deep. If you're planning to do 1-inch pours, use ThickSet epoxy. If you're planning on one 3-inch pour, you must use Fathom by TotalBoat. If you're not adding items or using a section of 2- to 3-inch-thick wood to create your riverbank, skip The Pour steps 1, 5, and 6 (page 163). You can use MakerPoxy for this project, but you'll have to pour it in *lots* of ⅛-inch layers. All the abovementioned thick pours require a minimum of 48 to 72 hours of **cure time** before demolding. You can demold Maker-Poxy 12 hours after your last pour.

Figure 1: MDF or HDPE Mold

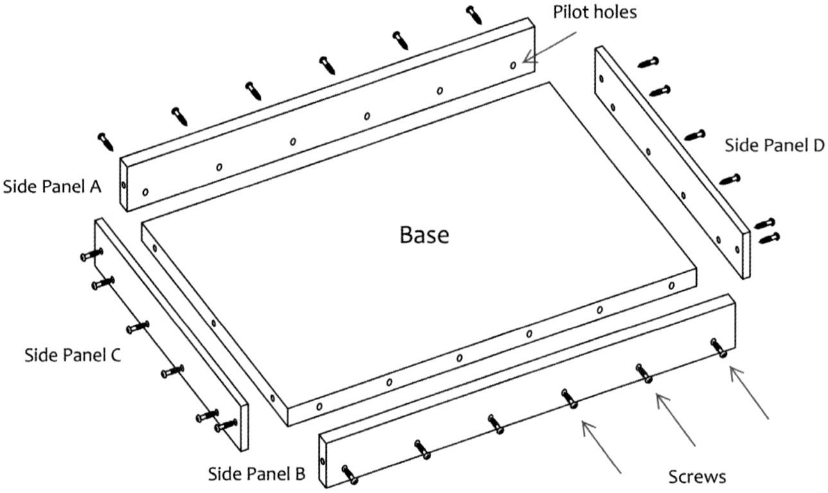

Pilot holes

Side Panel D

Side Panel A

Base

Side Panel C

Side Panel B

Screws

Figure 2

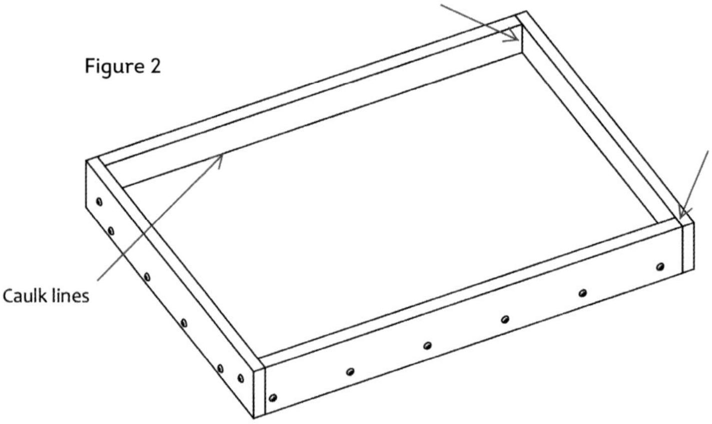

Caulk lines

The Mold

SUPPLIES & TOOLS

tape measure

pencil

1-inch-thick **melamine board**

table saw or circular saw

drill

pilot bit for screws

mold-release spray or nonstick **sheathing tape**

fast-drying caulk

caulk gun (optional)

½-inch screws

corner square

1.   Follow the Safety Requirements on page 84 and read all instructions before starting.

2.   Plan the size of the mold you want to use. Measure and mark the melamine 1 or 2 inches *longer* than needed in case you need to trim the cured epoxy because of defects or if **cupping** occurs.

> **NOTE:** Cupping happens when the mold or wood flexes and the epoxy pulls away from the edges.

3.   Using a table saw or circular saw, cut the five sides of the melamine box to the appropriate lengths.

4.   Drill pilot holes on all sides of the melamine or HDPE (see Figure 1 on page 160).

5.   If you're using a mold-release spray, proceed to step 6. If using nonstick sheathing tape, apply it to the base and side panels. Overlap the tape so no areas remain uncovered. Not using nonstick tape or a release agent correctly will allow epoxy to stick to the melamine, resulting in damage to the cured epoxy.

6.   Place a bead of fast-drying caulk on the edge of side panel A (see Figure 2 on page 160).

7.   Use a drill and ½-inch screws to secure panel A lightly to the base. Don't overtighten the screws. In the final step, you'll make sure they're snug.

CONTINUES

8. Place a bead of fast-drying caulk on the base of panel B (see Figure 2). Use the corner square to ensure the side panels sit flush and even.

9. Use the drill and ½-inch screws to secure panel A and panel B to the base.

10. Repeat steps 6 through 9 for the remaining side panels.

11. Line all the edges of the mold with fast-drying caulk (see Figure 2). This step works best if a small gap exists between the panels and the base so the caulk can get into every nook and cranny. (That's why it's important not to overtighten the screws.)

12. Once you've applied the caulk, tighten the screws. Use the corner square to confirm all the corners are sitting perfectly square (90 degrees). If the corners aren't sitting perfectly square and you can't adjust the mold, you'll still have an extra inch or two that you can cut off with a saw when you release the cured epoxy from the mold.

13. Allow the caulk to dry completely, ideally overnight, before moving on to the next step.

14. Thoroughly spray the mold with the release agent. If recommended by the manufacturer, allow it to dry, spray it again, and allow the second coat to dry.

The Pour

Once you've made the mold or assembled a store-bought one, it's time for a thick pour. Step 11 of the pour may require a decent amount of babysitting, so start early in the day.

SUPPLIES & TOOLS

rocks, sand, and other embedded objects

The Mold

ThickSet epoxy or Fathom

mixing cups

mixing sticks

blue mica powder

blue pigment paste

torch

1. Dry, seal, or otherwise prep any materials going in the mold. Set them aside.

2. Make sure the mold can sit in an undisturbed area, with proper airflow, for at least 36 hours. Confirm that the base of the mold is sitting level.

3. Calculate (JessCrow.com/epoxy-calculator), measure, and mix the appropriate amount of epoxy to cover the base of the mold by no more than 1 inch (⅛ inch if using MakerPoxy).

4. Add the blue mica powder or the blue pigment paste to the epoxy and mix completely. Note how much epoxy you've mixed and how much color you added. You'll need to repeat this exact step in step 10 or use clear epoxy to add depth.

5. Pour and use a torch to pop any bubbles.

6. Place the rocks in the mold, wiggling them around to make sure a decent amount of epoxy covers them or is in contact with them.

7. Sprinkle sand across the rocks and epoxy. Don't press the sand into the epoxy; it will settle as the epoxy cures.

8. Use a torch to pop any bubbles that have formed.

9. Cure for 12 to 18 hours or until the epoxy has the consistency of taffy.

10. Mix a matching batch of epoxy and color, as in steps 3 and 4, or use clear epoxy for depth.

11. Pour the epoxy into the mold.

12. Closely monitor the pour for any bubbles. If they arise, torch them. You may need to babysit the pour on and off for eight hours, so plan your day accordingly.

13. Cure for 24 to 48 hours, depending on the type of epoxy you've used.

CONTINUES

Demolding

SUPPLIES & TOOLS

drill or screwdriver

rubber mallet

shims

1. Remove the screws from the mold.

2. If the mold doesn't come away easily, loosen the sides by tapping them *gently* with a rubber mallet. Don't hit the top of the epoxy!

3. If the base has stuck to the epoxy, use shims to break the suction between the epoxy and the mold.

Assembly

Using 1-inch-thick maple or birch for the base adds texture and structural integrity to the table. Darker wood looks great, too. I like to use a leftover section of thick, interesting-looking plywood.

SUPPLIES & TOOLS

1-inch-thick plywood sheet, maple or birch

table saw or circular saw

sander

sandpaper, 60 and 80 grit

painter's tape

MakerPoxy

paint roller or paintbrush

two 2-by-4 boards

4 clamps

router

¼-inch round-over router bit

heat gun

wood stain in color of choice

four 16- to 18-inch coffee table legs

drill

½-inch screws to attach hardware

1. Cut the plywood with a table saw or circular saw to match the horizontal dimensions of the demolded coffee table.

2. Sand the top, bottom, and sides of the plywood with 60- then 80-grit sandpaper.

3. Tape the underside of the plywood.

4. Mix enough MakerPoxy to coat the top of the plywood, roughly ⅛ inch thick. This layer will act as glue so you need only enough to coat the surface.

5. Use a roller or brush to cover the plywood with epoxy completely. Avoid any bald spots.

6. Place the demolded table atop the coated plywood. Wiggle it back and forth to ensure good contact between the freshly poured epoxy and the table.

7. Lay the two 2-by-4 boards across the long edges of the coffee table and place the four clamps on either side.

8. Cure for 8 to 10 hours.

9. Remove the clamps.

10. Use the router fitted with a round-over bit to add a rounded edge to the top of the coffee table.

11. OPTIONAL: Use the router to add a rounded edge to the underside of the table.

12. Sand the top of the table with 60-grit sandpaper. Clean off any dust or grit.

CONTINUES

13. Continue sanding the top of the table with 80-grit sandpaper, carefully removing any swirls or marring. Clean any dust or other particulate from the surface.

14. Calculate, measure, and mix enough MakerPoxy to cover the entire surface and sides of the table with a clear, ⅛-inch pour.

15. Pour the epoxy onto the middle of the table and use a gloved hand to spread it around the top. Don't push the epoxy to the edges yet.

16. Use the heat gun to warm the epoxy gently.

17. Now, with a gloved hand, spread the epoxy to the edges.

18. Gently use the heat gun to level the epoxy and allow it to drip down the edges of the table.

19. Allow the epoxy to cure fully.

20. Flip the table over onto a padded surface and use the heat gun to remove the tape.

21. Sand down any remaining drips.

22. Seal the underside of the table. Allow it to dry.

23. Attach the legs to the underside of the table with a drill and ½-inch screws. Don't use screws longer than the plywood is thick or they'll poke through the epoxy.

IDEAS FOR VARIATIONS
- Serving trays
- Desks
- Larger tables
- Countertops

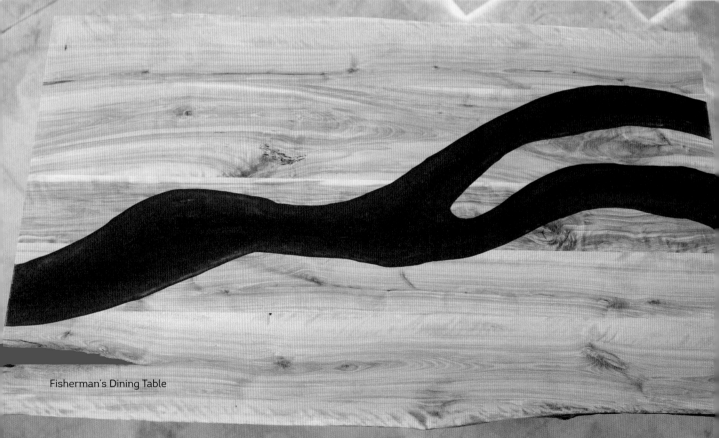

Fisherman's Dining Table

PROJECT
11

RIVER DINING TABLE

This dining table contains as many stories as that incredible fishing trip you took—or wish you could have taken! Filled with Alaskan red salmon swimming upstream, it reflects a day well spent.

If you're not familiar with a **Shaper Origin** handheld **CNC** or a stand-alone CNC, now's a fantastic time to explore the possibilities that these tools can offer. A CNC allows you to program and make precision cuts easily and safely, bringing your designs to life exactly as you envisioned them. If you're not ready to leap into a CNC, you can build this project without much fuss by using a handheld router and some creativity. If you have a slab large enough to accommodate a full-sized table, skip the building instructions in the handmade version and start cutting your river into the table.

To create a specific part of a real river for this project (not using a free-form design), you need to create a scalable vector graphic (**SVG**) that a CNC can read. It's a lot of letters, but the SVG is just the template that the CNC uses to cut the image you've selected. (CNCs also use other file formats, such as DXF, DWG, CDR. These formats are mostly universal but can be CNC specific. For this project, I'm using an SVG.) Find an image of the spot you want to re-create, run it through a CNC design program, and scale the image appropriately to fit on the slab. The Shaper Origin CNC comes with a program called ShaperHub, and most stand-alone CNCs work wonderfully with VCarve Pro or Aspire by Vec-

tric. The first cut will outline your design. Then you can switch to a handheld router to **clear** the slab, or a Shaper Origin CNC can do it all.

If you're not using a CNC, take your source image to a local print shop and have them print it out in ARCH E (36 x 48 inches; 914.4 x 1,219.2 mm) paper. You may need to have them create a tiled series for you if 36 x 48 inches isn't large enough to cover your table. Then use the printout as a template for your slab. Tape the template onto your slab and, using an awl, scratch the design onto the wood. Follow those lines with a handheld router. If the lines don't run deep or aren't easy enough to follow, trace them with a marker or other writing implement. White grease pens work great on dark wood, and you can wipe off any lines that you don't follow.

If you're going free-form with your river, the world is your oyster! Create any river you like with a drawing or freehand. Depending on the river you have in mind, you easily can swap in a different species of fish, too. If fish seem too intimidating, skip them and implement a design you like.

The thicker viscosity of MakerPoxy will give you more control over the pour and less worry because it won't leak all over the floor.

Store-Bought River Dining Table

wood slab, 39 x 72 x 2 inches (page 204)

rags

Shaper Origin CNC, stand-alone CNC, or handheld router with ¼-inch cutting bit and boring bit

clamps

shop vacuum

router (handheld)

shims

level

HVAC or aluminum

foil tape

MakerPoxy or ThickSet

mixing sticks

silicone brush (optional)

fine sand

small rocks (the smaller, the better)

white acrylic marker

paintbrushes

acrylic paints, dark green, light green, light red, dark red

sandpaper, 80, 120, and 180 grit

orbital sander or double drum sander

table legs

attachment bolts for legs

awl

drill

torch

rachet set (optional, to attach legs)

finishing oil (optional)

CONTINUES

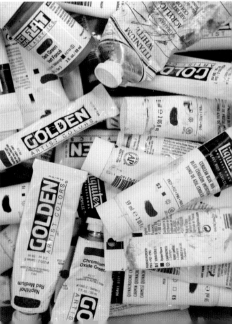

1. Follow the Safety Requirements on page 84 and read all instructions before starting.

2. Clean the wood slab with rags, removing all dust and oils.

3. Following the directions included with the Shaper Origin CNC, place the ShaperTape on the table with appropriate spacing or use proper lockdown techniques on the CNC bed.

4. Select your design and adjust as necessary. Select a final cut depth of ¼ inch.

5. Use the clamps to stabilize the slab.

6. With the Shaper Origin viewfinder or your CNC program, preview the design. Always double-check placement before cutting.

7. Start to cut the design. Periodically check the stability of the clamps and use a shop vac to remove any wood chips from the slab.

8. Finish the outline cut. When done, clean up any particulate and, if using a Shaper Origin, remove the tape from the tabletop or remove the table from the CNC bed, if using.

NOTE: If you are using the Shaper Origin CNC to remove all the wood, leave the tape. If using a router with a boring bit, remove the tape.

9. Using a handheld router, check the depth of the boring bit against the depth of the CNC cut. You want each cut to reach the same depth so you don't have to make more epoxy.

10. If not using a Shaper Origin CNC, carefully follow the outline of your river design to slowly remove the material.

11. Use a damp rag to clean off any sawdust and other particulate.

12. Move the slab to your pour station and level it with shims.

NOTE: Make sure the slab is perfectly level. If not, the epoxy will pool in places, resulting in an uneven pour.

13. OPTIONAL: To add depth, you can use rock- or "hammered-"style spray paint. To achieve this look, spray the selected type of spray paint within the area you cut out using your router or CNC. Then allow to fully dry before moving on to the next step.

14. Tear off enough HVAC or aluminum foil tape and apply it to the ends of the slab where you routed the river. The tape will act as a dam to keep the epoxy from flowing off the slab.

15. Calculate, measure, and mix the appropriate amount of MakerPoxy for the depth of the cut.

16. Slowly pour a thin layer, ⅛ inch or less, of MakerPoxy down the length of the void. This thin layer serves only as "glue" for the rocks and sand in the following steps.

17. Using a silicone brush or a clean mixing stick, spread the epoxy to cover the bottom of the void. Remember, this layer functions just as glue, so don't pour deep.

18. Coat the sides of the void, too, which will seal the wood, reducing the number of bubbles that may arise when you do larger pours later in the process.

CONTINUES

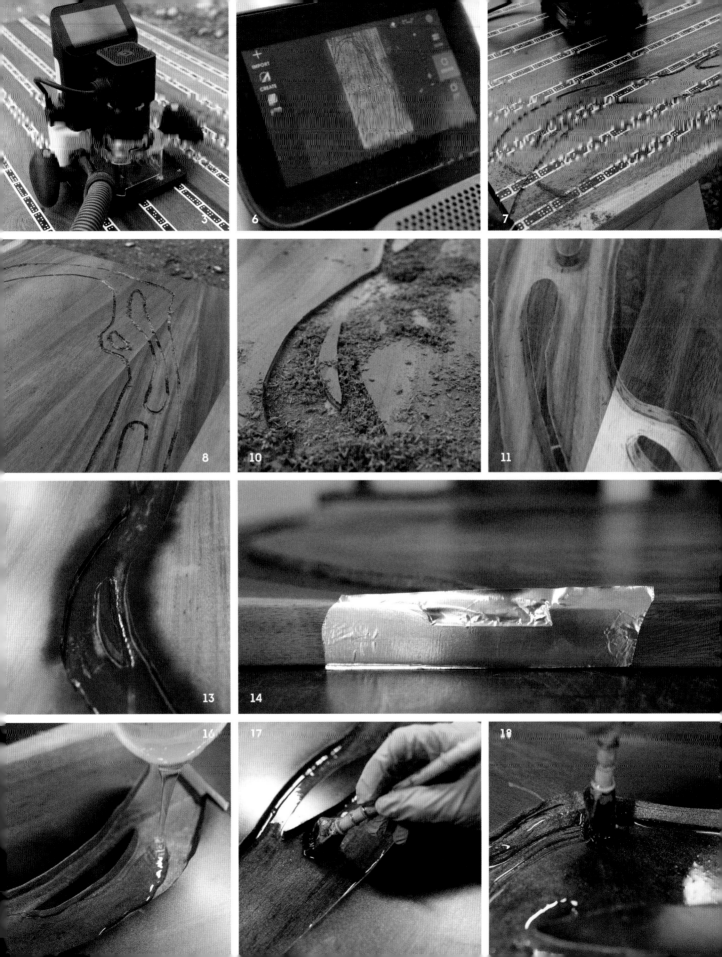

19. Sprinkle the sand into the prepared void, followed by the rocks. Make sure the rocks don't rise above the ¼-inch line that you've cut. Cover the entire base of the void with them. If any sand or rocks wind up on top of the slab, you can clean them off with a rag.

20. Cure for 6 to 8 hours.

21. With a white acrylic marker, draw the spines of the fish. Use 1- to 1½-inch lines for fin placement and to outline bodies. This is layer 2.

22. Using dark green acrylic paint and a small paintbrush, make small, rice-shaped brushstrokes on both sides of the white lines to create pectoral fins.

23. Calculate, measure, and mix just enough epoxy to pour a thin layer, ⅛ inch or less, down the length of the void.

24. Cure for 6 to 8 hours.

25. With the white acrylic marker, draw the spines of the fish for layer 3.

26. With light and dark green acrylic paint, make strokes larger than a grain of rice on layer 1 to form additional pectoral fins.

27. With light and dark red acrylic paint, create scales for the fish in layer 3.

28. Repeat steps 22 and 23.

NOTE: The images produced in an MRI scan are called planes. One of those planes is called the transverse, or axial, plane. In layman's terms, it gives a view of the body, slice by slice. For this project, you'll be working from the bottom layer up, capturing the look of the fish the same way an MRI would, but on a flat plane, like this:

LAYER 7: final epoxy pour
LAYER 6: epoxy pour
LAYER 5: red scales of fish in layer 4, epoxy
LAYER 4: green bodies of fish in layer 3, red scales of fish in layer 2, epoxy

LAYER 3: spines and pectoral fins of the second half of the fish, green layer on the bodies of fish in layer 2, epoxy
LAYER 2: spines and pectoral fins of the first half of the fish, epoxy
LAYER 1: epoxy, sand, and rocks (steps 15 through 18)

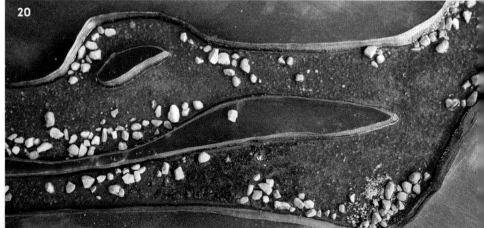

29. Using the green acrylic paints, paint strokes larger than a grain of rice to form pectoral fins on the fish in layer 3.

30. Repeat steps 22 and 23.

31. With the red acrylic paints, ... for the fish in layer 4.

32. Repeat steps 22 and 23.

33. Repeat step 22 for the final epoxy layer.

34. Cure final layer for 18 to 24 hours.

CONTINUES

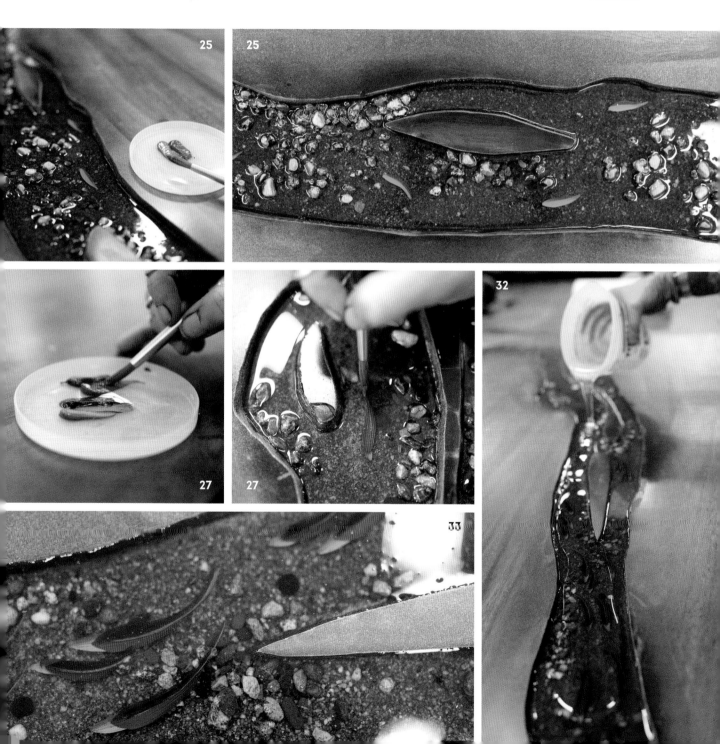

35. Remove the HVAC or aluminum foil tape. If residue remains, sand it off with 120-grit sandpaper.

36. Using an orbital sander or a double drum sander, sand the entire slab with 80-grit sandpaper.

37. Work your way up through 120 grit and 180 grit. At 180, pay particular attention to swirl marks. If you see any, reduce the pressure from the sander and make sure you're using clean sander pads.

38. Clean off any particulate or dust.

39. For a matte finish, use a hybrid finishing oil and allow it to cure. For a glossy finish, do a final clear pour.

40. Gather the mounting hardware and appropriate tools for the table legs. (This slab uses Nutsert rivet nuts and the corresponding bolts.)

41. Using an awl, mark where the nuts and bolts should go, then drill a pilot hole in each location.

42. Using the appropriate-sized bit, follow the pilot hole to drill a deeper hole for each of the nuts. Insert the nuts.

43. Attach the legs to the slab using the mounting hardware.

Handmade River Dining Table

SUPPLIES & TOOLS

slabs of wood in species of choice, at least 2 inches thick ("8/4"), completely dry

chisel and hammer or **drawknife**

planer (optional)

track saw or table saw

tape measure

pencil

domino joiner (page 204) or **biscuit joiner**

dominoes or biscuits

wood glue

table clamps (as needed)

CA glue or 4-minute epoxy (optional)

level

double drum sander or hand sander

sandpaper, 60, 80, and 120 grit

router

shop vacuum

wood paste (optional)

chip brush (optional)

MakerPoxy or ThickSet

acrylic paint in color(s) of choice (optional)

HVAC or aluminum foil tape

mica powder or **liquid pigment**, blue

stickers or stamps to create design elements

silicone brush (optional)

table legs

mounting hardware for table legs

awl

drill

torch

rachet set (optional, to attach legs)

finishing oil (optional)

1. Follow the Safety Requirements on page 84 and read all instructions before starting.

2. Using a chisel and hammer or drawknife, remove the bark from the slabs.

3. OPTIONAL. Use a planer to even out or smooth the slabs to the exact thickness you want.

4. If you're creating a live-edge table, determine which edges look most natural or have the most character. Mark them accordingly. Lay them on the floor for a bird's-eye view of how they might look as a tabletop.

5. Use a track or table saw to make rip cuts (parallel to the woodgrain) to cut the edges off the slabs. Don't cut off the live edges.

6. Cut off one side of each slab to domino or biscuit-join it to the straight edge of the adjoining slab.

7. Lay out the newly created boards.

8. Measure and mark where the domino or biscuit joints will go.

9. Use either your domino joiner or biscuit joiner to create the domino or biscuit pocket.

10. Repeat step 8 along the length of all boards being joined.

CONTINUES

11. Insert the appropriate joining device and test fit the table.

12. If the test fit works properly, add lots of wood glue to the boards and quickly pull them all together with table clamps. Allow to dry.

13. Fill any knots or gaps in the wood with CA glue or 4-minute epoxy. Allow to dry or cure completely.

14. After the glue or epoxy has dried, ensure that the table is level. If it has any high spots, use a double drum sander or a hand sander to remove them *carefully* without making any more high or low spots in the wood.

> **NOTE:** For this step, you can use a CNC with a flattening bit if one is available.

15. If you haven't already, trim the ends of the slabs.

16. Using a pencil, outline where you want your river to flow on the table. Make sure you're happy with the location. Once you route it, correcting it will prove challenging. Mark any islands or areas you want to keep so you don't cut them out by accident.

17. Using a handheld router set to the appropriate depth, carve out the river section. Don't go more than ¼ inch deep into the slabs and *don't cut all the way through the table.*

18. Clean up all debris and particulate with a shop vac.

19. OPTIONAL. Apply wood paste to the bottom of the void you routed, creating a textured base by applying the paste unevenly.

20. Use the chip brush to paint the bottom of the river with acrylic paint. Allow it to dry.

21. Tear off enough HVAC or aluminum foil tape to cover the cut ends of the river section on the table. The tape will act as a dam to keep the epoxy from flowing off the slab.

22. Calculate, measure, and mix the appropriate amount of MakerPoxy for the section of river you've cut ¼ inch deep.

23. Tint the epoxy with blue mica powder or liquid pigment.

24. Pour the epoxy into the river section at a depth of ⅛ to ¼ inch.

25. Cure for 5 to 8 hours.

26. Leave the river plain or add details, such as vinyl stickers or stamps, if desired. Make sure any stamps are dry and stickers are pressed down fully before proceeding.

27. Pour more epoxy down the center of the previous pour. Use a gloved hand or a silicone brush to push the epoxy into all areas.

28. Repeat steps 24 through 27 until the epoxy sits slightly higher than the cut sections of river.

29. Remove the HVAC or aluminum foil tape from the table edges.

30. Use a double drum sander or hand sand the entire top of the table to produce a level finish.

> **NOTE:** Some woodshops have a large machine called a Timesaver, which can plane and sand an entire table in one pass. If a shop in your area has one of these amazing machines, consider having this service done. The drive there probably will take more time than the process itself, and it's worth the money.

CONTINUES

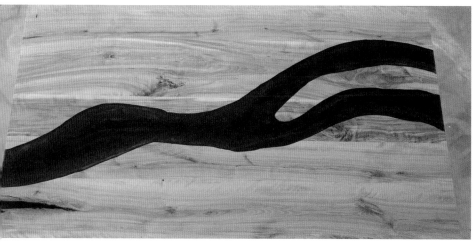

31. For a matte finish, use a hybrid finishing oil and allow it to cure. For a glossy finish, do a final clear pour.

32. Depending on the type of legs you've made or purchased, collect the appropriate mounting hardware and tools. For this slab, I use Nutsert rivet nuts and the corresponding bolts to attach the legs.

33. Using an awl, mark where the nuts and bolts should go, then drill a pilot hole in each location.

34. Using the appropriate-sized bit, follow the pilot hole to drill a deeper hole for each of the nuts. Insert the nuts.

35. Attach the legs to the slab using the mounting hardware.

IDEAS FOR VARIATIONS
- Box inlays
- Dresser tops
- Wall art
- Desks
- Partitions

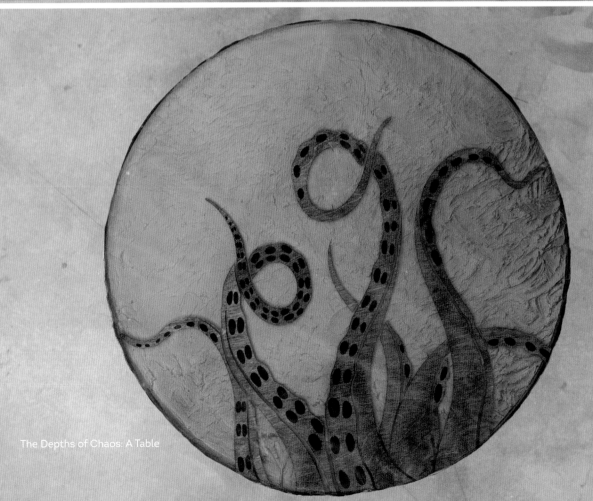

The Depths of Chaos: A Table

CHAOS TABLE

When left to my own devices, I like to make things as complex as possible. In the middle of a project, I'll think of three more ways to do it. This mindset helps troubleshooting, but it's not so cool with responsibilities to fulfill and deadlines to meet. Chaos, I tell you, pure chaos. In one big package, this table design encapsulates all the chaos of epoxy resin, multiple design elements, and many of the skills you've learned in this book.

If you don't have a laser cutter, a **CNC** router, a jigsaw (and a lot of patience), or another means of cutting a layer from a ⅛-inch-thick piece of wood, a lot of folks out there do. Ask! Also consider looking for a local maker space, a co-op where you can rent equipment for an hour and get to know others learning how to use the same or similar equipment.

This project uses MakerPoxy for its clarity and thickness, qualities integral to working with the many layers of a project this size. It contains just one version of the tutorial because I bought a round from a hardware store. For maximum chaos, fashion one yourself by modifying the steps to make a round for the End Table (page 146). You can find file information for the octopus in the Resources section (page 204).

Let the chaos begin!

Chaos Table

SUPPLIES & TOOLS

36-inch diameter wooden
tabletop (page 204)

UV resin and **UV light bar** or
CA glue (optional)

painter's tape

level

putty knife

1 or 2 pints Painter's Putty '53' (page 204)

spray paint, light blue, light green,
dark green, dark blue

trash can dolly (optional)

chip brushes (optional)

MakerPoxy

HVAC or aluminum foil tape

heat gun

torch

sheet of Baltic birch, 38 x 38 x $\frac{1}{8}$ inches

laser cutter, CNC router, or jigsaw

clear wood stain or shellac

CA glue or 4-minute epoxy

paintbrush

acrylic paint, black and gray

sander

80-grit **sandpaper**

mixing cup

fine sand

mixing sticks

level

drill

sixteen $\frac{1}{2}$-inch screws

eight 1-inch black pipe base
flanges (page 204)

four 1-x-16-inch sections of
black pipe (page 204)

CONTINUES

1. Follow the Safety Requirements on page 84 and read all instructions before starting.

2. Check the round for any cracks or knots. If you spot any, use UV resin or CA glue to fill them.

3. Tape the underside of the round and level it.

4. Use a putty knife or a gloved hand to spread Painter's Putty '53' across the round.

5. Create peaks and valleys by pressing into the putty with a gloved hand and lifting it immediately. Drag your hand across the putty, circling the round, to create a vortex pattern.

6. Once you're happy with the putty, allow it to dry overnight. It contains a lot of water and needs ample time to release that moisture.

7. Spray-paint the whole surface light blue.

> **TIP:** To give the putty-covered round a lot of color depth and dimension in the following steps, you need to move around it a lot or have a means of spinning it easily. Create a "turntable" by using a trash can dolly.

8. Holding the can of light green spray paint at a 30-degree angle, spray the bottom section, keeping the light blue in some sections while adding green tones.

9. Move either to the left or right of the round and repeat the prior step with the dark green spray paint. Don't cover the whole round; you want some light blue to remain visible.

10. Moving to the opposite side of the round, hold the can of dark blue spray paint almost level with the table. With wide, sweeping motions, spray a thin layer of paint. When you turn the table or move to the other side, it should look almost as if you didn't use any dark blue paint. But on the opposite side dark blue should appear on the putty peaks.

11. Repeat steps 8 through 10 until you paint the round completely. Various colors of spray paint should highlight all the peaks and valleys of putty. Allow the round to dry overnight.

12. Calculate, measure, and mix enough MakerPoxy to cover the entire round in a layer ⅛ inch deep.

13. Carefully pour the epoxy onto the middle of the round and gently move it around using a chip brush or a gloved hand. Move very delicately to avoid shifting or breaking the fragile putty.

14. Cure for 6 to 9 hours.

15. Wrap the HVAC or aluminum foil tape around the entire round. Make sure the tape attaches above the lip as well as on the edge of the round. You want to have a dam in which to capture the epoxy.

CONTINUES

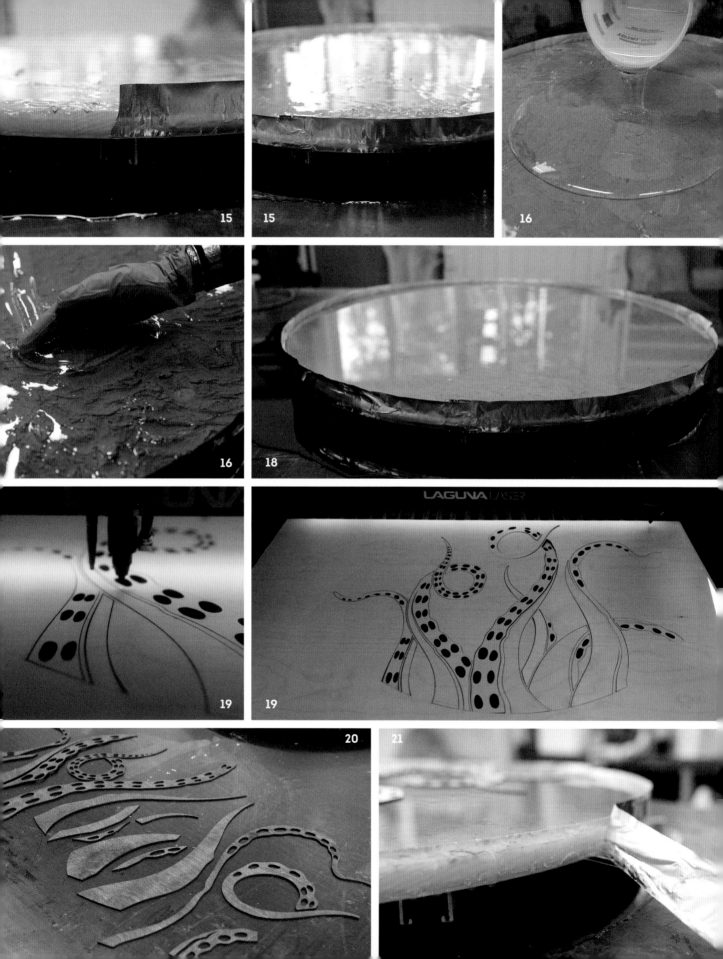

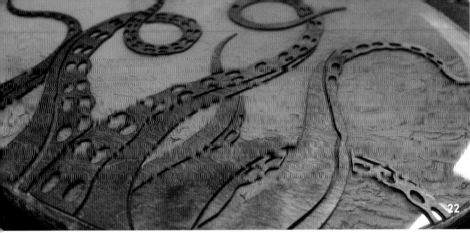
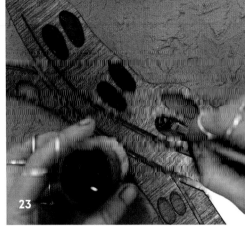
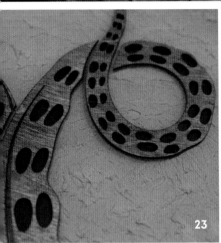
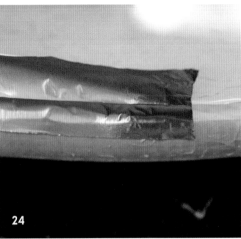
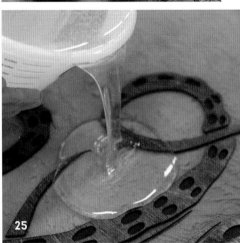

16. Mix another batch of MakerPoxy to cover the round in a layer ¼ inch deep—but no more than that! Pour and spread to the edges.

> **TIP:** You're pushing the limits of Maker-Poxy, so be mindful of this step. The epoxy should cover the putty peaks completely. If it doesn't, *don't* add more. Fully cure the epoxy and pour another layer.

17. Use a heat gun to move the epoxy around and a torch to pop any bubbles that appear.

18. Cure for 6 to 8 hours.

19. While the epoxy is curing, cut an octopus shape from the sheet of Baltic birch with a laser cutter, CNC router, or jigsaw.

20. Using either clear wood stain or shellac, seal the back and front of the octopus cut-out. Do this repeatedly to make sure you seal the wood *completely*. If you don't, it will bubble something awful.

21. Remove the HVAC or aluminum foil tape.

22. Align the curve of the table with the curved edge of the octopus. Use CA glue or 4-minute epoxy to attach the octopus to the table. Thoroughly spread the adhesive over the bottom of the octopus cutout. You don't want any air in any gaps for the next pour.

23. Brush black acrylic paint on the suckers of the octopus. Allow to dry.

CONTINUES

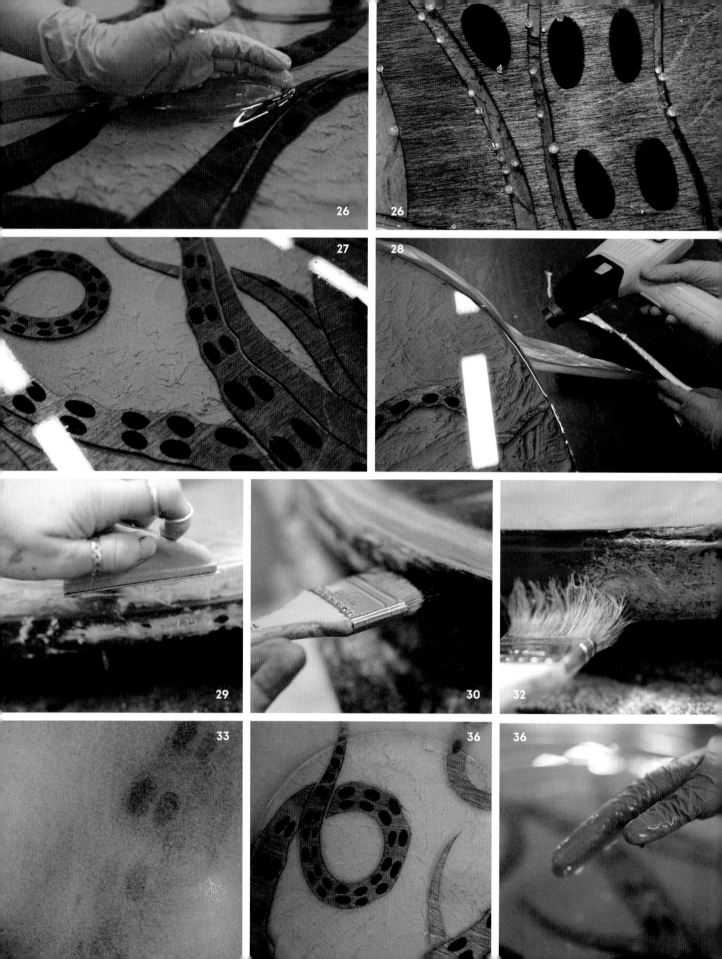

24. Reapply HVAC or aluminum foil tape around the entire round, as in step 15. Don't worry about wrapping it perfectly. Bumps add to the effectiveness of the design. The bumpier, the better!

25. Calculate, measure, and mix another batch of MakerPoxy to cover the surface of the round and the octopus. Pour.

26. Move the epoxy around with a gloved hand or heat gun and torch any bubbles that appear.

27. Cure for 6 to 8 hours.

28. Remove the HVAC or aluminum foil tape. Use a heat gun if necessary.

29. If the epoxy has a sharp lip, gently remove it with a sander and 80-grit sandpaper. Don't worry about marring the surface of the round when you sand because you still have another pour. If the epoxy is uneven but not sharp, move to the next step.

30. Brush black acrylic paint around the outside edge of the round. Allow to dry.

31. In a mixing cup, add gray acrylic paint and some of the fine sand. Mix the paint and sand until well incorporated, making sure you have enough to go all the way around the outside edge of the round.

32. Paint the outside edge of the round with the paint and sand mixture. You may have to use a gloved hand or a chip brush to press the mixture onto the round. Allow to dry.

33. Using a sander with 80-grit sandpaper, sand the top of the round. Keep the sander flat to remove any dry paint drips, but don't let it touch the edges of the round. The octopus will fade, but that's OK. You'll bring it back to life with the final pour.

34. For the final pour, watch out for bugs or other unwanted objects and make sure the round is level.

35. Calculate, measure, and mix enough MakerPoxy for a pour 1/8 inch deep.

36. Starting in the center of the round, pour the epoxy and use a gloved hand to spread it out.

37. Spread the epoxy over the edges of the table. The edges should appear bumpy and uneven to mimic stone, an effect you intentionally created by repeatedly applying and removing the HVAC or aluminum foil tape.

38. With a gloved hand, press the epoxy to the edges. Allow it to cascade over them.

39. If any bubbles appear, pop them with your heat gun.

40. Cure for 12 to 18 hours.

41. Flip the round over onto a soft surface and use the heat gun to remove the tape from the underside.

42. Seal the underside of the round with wood stain or shellac.

43. Using the drill and screws, attach the black pipe base flanges to the table.

44. Twist the black pipe sections onto the base flanges.

45. Twist the remaining black pipe base flanges to the bottom of the black pipe.

CONTINUES

IDEAS FOR VARIATIONS
The Depths of Chaos know endless possibilities.

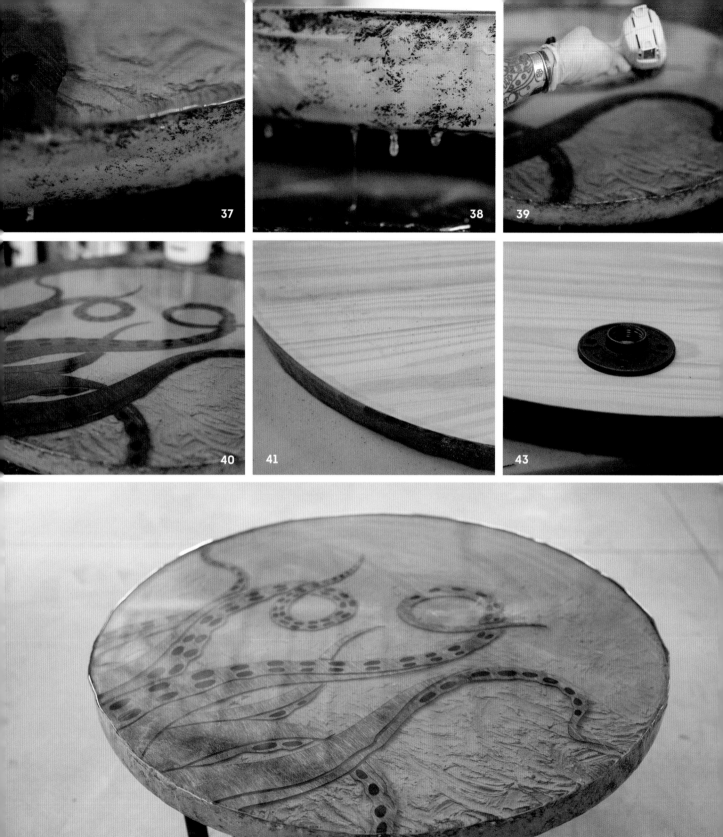

ACKNOWLEDGMENTS

Writing any book is a massive undertaking, but writing a book on a subject that no one else has tackled in quite the same way makes for an even greater feat—at least for me. When I undertook writing this book, I underestimated the amount of time it would take from my family, friends, and work. Projects that I've done hundreds of times, usually within a few days, took weeks to complete and document over the course of more than a year. Through it all, my family, colleagues, and social media friends and followers remained steadfast, holding me up. I cannot thank you enough for that. In these days of instant gratification, it's a blessing to have folks hang around, "on hold," while I muddle through all the moving parts of my life.

Family. We've been through a lot and have a lot more to go through. Being strong is in our genes, but so are kindness, compassion, encouragement, and respect. You've shown me all of that while I've worked through this incredible undertaking. "I love you" doesn't cover it.

T, I cannot express how proud of you I am for what you've overcome. Mastering your future versus living in the past is hard work. You are a role model to those around us.

N, you make sunshine when there isn't any and rainbows when you can't. Smiles are your love language, and your ability to make others feel that is unsurpassed.

S, strength comes in many forms. If we all could learn how to overcome fear with the grace and beauty you possess, the world would be a much better place.

I, unapologetically you. Filled with determination to right the wrongs of the world, balanced with superhuman bravery. You will do great things; you already are.

Ruthann, love you, and I will have your swing ready in the shop.

Kristin, without your support and "I believe in you, sister!" attitude, this project would have been a lot harder, if not impossible. You, Mike, and the Total-Boat team had faith in me even when I'd lost it. When we first started talking about MakerPoxy, we had big dreams, goals, and lofty aspirations. Now we're surrounded by an amazing community of makers, artists, and builders who share the same dreams, goals, and aspirations. We're a growing, self-chosen family who are educating, encouraging, and showing others how to build amazing creations.

Monte, you let me get your entire classroom sticky with my first teaching experience. You never made me feel bad as I learned how to be a teacher (oftentimes at the expense of your store!). Remember, struggling is not the same as failing.

Mike, from the moment we met, "how to do things safely" was a hot topic we both were passionate about. Your wisdom and enthusiasm to help others succeed (in a safe manner) inspire not only me but also the millions of people who watch you. Your hard-fought journey goes way beyond helping folks rebuild their homes; it rebuilds folks' faith in humanity. I am honored to call you "friend."

Andrew, if the world only knew what a soft heart you have, your cover would be blown. You do your job in a way that long has been forgotten: with dedication, determination, loyalty, and the will to see it through, regardless of outside notions.

Adam, Jennifer, and James, you rock! One down and, patience willing, more to come.

Last but certainly not least, my students, online community, and friends, your input and participation throughout this journey of teaching and creating have brought this book to life. The questions you challenge me with, the ideas you bring to the table in the classroom, and your willingness to work through less-than-ideal situations have inspired me constantly to ask myself questions such as *How can I make all of this easier for you?* Without your desire to learn, grow, and be more, this book never would have come to fruition. It came to life not only from your desires but also from mine to build more than furniture.

Always remember to embrace your weird!

GLOSSARY

1:1 formula: A formula composed of two quantities that are measured in exactly the same proportion.

Air cleaner: Any device that removes impurities from the air, particularly suspended particles.

Air-exchange system: This type of fan pulls air into a room with one blade while pushing it out with another.

Aluminum foil tape: A stiff tape that combines flexibility with the protective qualities of aluminum.

Ambient temperature: The temperature of the air or any material in contact with the epoxy. It varies by location and time of year.

Angle grinder: A power tool used for grinding, cutting, polishing, etc.

Biscuit joiner (biscuit jointer, plate joiner): This woodworking tool cuts notches into two pieces of wood so they fit together. A glue biscuit goes into each piece of wood, joining the two, resulting in a reliable joint that prevents lateral movement.

Bonding primer: Formulated to adhere to a variety of difficult **substrates**, especially highly porous ones, this primer reduces the need for sanding by providing a thick, smooth coating.

BPA (bisphenol A): A chemical compound primarily used in manufacturing plastics.

CA glue (cyanoacrylate): Also called ethyl cyanoacrylate, super glue, or instant adhesive, this popular, clear, quick-drying, strong-bonding adhesive takes the shape of a polymer (plastic) resin in its cured form.

Cane: Rods or stacks of a colored medium, often glass or polymer clay, that run the entire length of a project. Cutting a cross-section reveals a pattern.

Casting: When mixed resin pours into a space, usually a mold, and cures.

Casting epoxy: This resin used to create 3D shapes in a **mold** cures to a clear, glassy finish with minimal shrinkage.

Chemical reaction: A transformation that occurs when two or more substances combine to form a new one.

Chip brush: This solidly made brush resists solvents and won't leave bristles on a coated surface. Ideal for applying glue, stain, paint remover, oils, etc.

Clear/clearing: Using a large router bit to clear a large section of wood by removing bark, for example, then using a smaller bit for any further smoothing or detail work.

CNC (computer numerical control): An electronic machine that uses computer software to cut many types of materials, including wood, plastic, aluminum, and high-density foam.

Corner square (square tool): A tool to check the accuracy of a 90-degree angle before marking and cutting materials or drilling holes.

Cupping: When wood or a **mold** flexes—in response to moisture, for example—epoxy pulls from the edges or sides, creating a curved shape, like the inside of a cup.

Cure time: The length of time it takes epoxy resin to dry and harden completely.

Data sheet (material safety data sheet, MSDS, safety data sheet, SDS): This manufacturer-provided document contains critically important technical information on chemicals, including their composition, proper storage, use, safe disposal, and potential hazards.

Deburring tool: This tool removes rough, uneven edges from epoxy resin projects, creating a smooth, even effect.

Dehumidifier: This machine removes water vapor, or humidity, from the air.

Dirty pour: A pouring technique in which different colors can be mixed in separate cups and then blended together on a surface. Alternatively, different colors can be added to one cup and then poured.

Doming: Using resin to create a dome on a surface, or the type of resin suitable for doming.

Domino Joiner: This specialized piece of equipment joins two pieces of wood together in a process called mortise and tenon joinery, one of the simplest and strongest methods. It cuts grooves for domino-shaped biscuits and cuts in the same way as a **biscuit joiner**.

Double drum sander: This machine sands with two grits in a single pass, reducing time spent sanding and preventing burning, gouging, and other damage.

Drawknife: This hand tool shapes wood by removing shavings. It consists of a blade with a handle at each end and can be used in many ways, including stripping off bark.

Exothermic reaction: This release of heat occurs when epoxy and hardener combine. The more they mix, the more heat they generate and the faster the epoxy will cure, making it difficult to manage.

Finishing oil: An oil-based finish used in woodworking.

Flash cure: This **chemical reaction** between resin and hardener generates heat as epoxy cures. If you mix too much epoxy and leave it sitting for more than the prescribed amount of time, it will start to boil, bubble, and smoke, ultimately leading to an uneven cure.

Flood coat: A clear **topcoat** of epoxy resin.

Food-contact surface: Any surface that may touch food directly.

Food safe: A term that designates a food-grade material suitable for its intended use, such as a plate for serving food. The term *doesn't* mean that the FDA or other regulatory body approves such items for use in or around food in all possible conditions.

Full cure: When epoxy cures fully, the resin and hardener have reacted completely with each other to form a solid, inflexible material suitable for sanding or shaping.

Glassing: This coating gives surfaces a clear, high-gloss finish and durability.

Grit size: This **sandpaper** measure notes the number of abrasive particles per square inch.

Hand layup (wet layup): This manual technique uses liquid epoxy resin to position layers of lamination in a **mold** until achieving the desired thickness or shape.

HDPE (high-density polyethylene): A hard, versatile plastic to which epoxy doesn't stick.

Heat gun: This handheld, flameless device produces heat, typically at two temperature settings ranging from low heat (392°/200°) to high heat (572°/300°). It causes epoxy to expand, thereby removing bubbles, and creates an even surface that cures better and proves more durable.

High-Performance epoxy: This hard, durable, all-purpose gloss epoxy works best with surfaces where resistance to chemicals and abrasion is essential.

Holographic paint: This alcohol-based paint contains microparticles that reflect light and produce iridescent rainbow colors and a metallic finish.

Holographic shrink-wrap film: A thin, flexible film made of plastic and nylon that has been micro-embossed with patterns and images, creating a 3D effect or rainbow coloring that resembles a hologram.

Kerf cut: The thickness of the cut that a blade makes in a piece of wood. "Kerf" also describes the thickness of the blade itself, such as a fine-cut blade with a kerf width of 0.087 inches (2.21 mm).

Lacing: A lace-like pattern created when a **heat gun** pushes pigmented resin at an angle.

Large pour: Generally any epoxy resin pour more than 36 fluid ounces or 2.2 pounds (1 kg).

Lathe: This versatile cutting tool shapes wood into furniture, such as tabletops, chair legs, etc.

Layers/layering: A second coating of epoxy, poured after the first coat feels a little sticky (usually after 4 to 6 hours), to build the preferred depth.

Liquid latex: This multiuse liquid rubber makes flexible, durable **molds** and can protect the underside of projects from wandering epoxy drips.

Liquid pigment: An insoluble colorant suspended in a liquid carrier, used as a coloring agent in epoxy resin.

MDF: Medium-density fiberboard.

Medium cure: A hardener that provides a medium-speed **cure time** for epoxy resin at room temperature.

Melamine: A plastic used chiefly for laminated coatings.

Melamine board: The plastic used in the laminated coating on **melamine** boards makes them highly durable, scratch resistant, waterproof, stain resistant, and easy to clean.

Mica powder: This natural mineral colors epoxy resin. Shimmery, iridescent particles in the powder create stunning effects when the resin cures.

Mil: $^1/_{1000}$ inch, a unit of measure for the thickness of plastic; 6-mil plastic offers extra-heavy-duty protection.

Mold: A hollow container, usually with a specific form, in which to pour epoxy resin. As it cures, the resin assumes the shape of the mold. Resin-crafting molds most commonly consist of plastic or silicone.

Mold-release spray: An airborne chemical that prevents epoxy resin from sticking to **molds**, making it easy to demold them.

Open time: See "pot life."

Painter's tape: This thin tape, often called "masking tape," is pressure sensitive and easy to remove.

Part A, Part B: Part A is usually resin and Part B normally is the hardener. Always double-check the manufacturer's **data sheet**.

Pen blank: A small piece of wood, typically 5 x ¾ x ¾, +/- ⅛ inch, commonly used to make pens.

Pigment: This solid colorant typically results in more opaque transparency than a solid pigment suspended in a liquid carrier. In smaller quantities, it can look translucent. Solid pigment may take more effort to disperse evenly in epoxy and can settle out of the epoxy if the pot life is long enough.

Pot life (open time, pot time): It begins when the mixing of resin and hardener is complete and ends when the mixture has become unsuitable for application due to inadequate mixing or too much time sitting after mixing but before pouring.

Pot time: See "pot life."

Powered air-purifying respirator (PAPR): This respirator consists of a headgear-and-fan assembly that removes harmful elements from ambient air, delivering clean, filtered air to the user's mouth and nose. Sometimes called positive-pressure masks, blower units, or blowers.

PPE: Personal protective equipment, including safety goggles, a respirator, gloves, protective clothing, and footwear.

Pressure pot: Chamber used for pressure casting, a process in which a resin casting or **mold** is placed in a chamber attached to an air compressor. The compressor forces air into the pressure pot, eliminating bubbles. The resin remains in the pot for the entire curing time.

Ratio: The relative proportion between two or more elements. For epoxy and hardener, the ratios could be 1:1 (one part resin to one part hardener), 2:1 (two parts resin to one part hardener), etc.

Safe for contact with food: An inert plastic, epoxy resin is considered safe only for *occasional, short-term* contact with food after it has cured fully. Keep all food and beverages well away from resin and hardener before curing completes. Epoxy resin is never edible or potable in any form.

Sander: This handheld tool creates smooth surfaces. Common types include orbital, disc, and finish sanders.

Sandpaper: Measured by **grit size**, or the number of abrasive particles per square inch, from 60 to 400. Lower grit numbers feel coarser and scrape materials more quickly. The higher the number, the finer the abrasive.

Seize: When epoxy suddenly loses its pliability.

Self-leveling formula: This formula of epoxy automatically levels itself to a ⅛-inch depth. It cures to a hard, clear surface resistant to water and scratches.

Shaper Origin CNC: This portable, easy-to-use handheld CNC router provides computer-guided precision cutting.

Sheathing tape: This specialized tape creates a water-resistant seal and performs well across a wide range of temperatures.

Side-by-side pour: A technique for pouring one section of epoxy (color A) and then immediately pouring another section of epoxy (color B) next to color A.

Silicone caulk: Due to its flexibility, it is less likely to crack and peel than other caulking, making it a frequently used sealant to achieve a waterproof, protective joint seal.

Small pour: Generally, any epoxy resin pour fewer than 36 fluid ounces or 2.2 pounds (1 kg).

Substrate: The base of any project or surface, such as wood or an existing countertop.

SVG (scalable vector graphic): An image format that a **CNC** router uses for precision cutting.

Tang: A tang or shank is the back portion of the blade or shaft of a tool. It extends into or connects with the handle of a knife or screwdriver, for example.

Thermal expansion: This phenomenon occurs when an increase in temperature causes materials to become larger.

Toast/toasting: When a **heat gun** applies too much heat to epoxy resin, causing it to gel and become unworkable.

Topcoat: The final layer applied in a project as a protective layer, including a **flood coat** of epoxy or wood stain.

Torch: This handheld, gas-powered tool quickly pops bubbles in epoxy resin.

Tuck tape: This tape doesn't stick to epoxy resin, so it can keep pours in place or line **molds** to make demolding easier.

UHMW (ultra-high molecular weight): An extremely tough, versatile plastic with high resistance to abrasion and wear, making it a popular choice for applications that require durability. Epoxy resin doesn't stick to it.

UV light apparatus or bar: This specialized lamp cures ultraviolet resin via a photochemical reaction that causes the epoxy to harden.

Vacuum pot: In **mold** making and casting, a vacuum pot or chamber eliminates air bubbles in hard-setting materials.

VOCs (volatile organic compounds): Certain processes or products, such as paints, paint stripper, wood preservatives, aerosol sprays, and solvents, emit these compounds into the air. VOCs are harmful, and some can cause cancer.

Wet layup: See "hand layup."

RESOURCES

For a complete list of resources, visit
JessCrow.com/resources

PPE

APRON
Leather by Dragonfly
LeatherByDragonfly.com, JessCrow.com/resources

EYE-FLUSH KIT AND EYEWASH STATION
drugstore, pharmacy, big-box store, home improvement store

FOOTWEAR
KEEN Vista Energy (Carbon Fiber Toe)
KeenFootwear.com, JessCrow.com/resources

GLOVES
disposable latex, nitrile, or vinyl
drugstore, pharmacy, big-box store, home improvement store

GOGGLES
drugstore, pharmacy, big-box store, home improvement store

RESPIRATOR
GVS SPR457 Elipse P100 Dust Half Mask Respirator
JessCrow.com/resources

SUPPLIES

ALCOHOL, DENATURED
big-box store, home improvement store

ALCOHOL, ISOPROPYL (RUBBING)
drugstore, pharmacy, big-box store, home improvement store

BONDING PRIMER
big-box store, home improvement store

CLEANING CLOTHS
big-box store, home improvement store

EPOXY, MAKERPOXY, AND OTHER FORMULAS
TotalBoat.com, TotalBoat.com/MakerPoxy, JessCrow.com/resources

EPOXY REMOVER
big-box store, home improvement store

FINISHES (SPECIALTY)
ProCoat UnoCoat and Rubio Monocoat Pure Finish
JessCrow.com/resources

FINISHING COMPOUNDS OR POLISHES
big-box store, home improvement store
Liquid latex

CREATURE LIQUID LATEX (CLEAR)
art store, costume store, JessCrow.com/resources

MDF
Home improvement store

MICA POWDERS
Black Diamond pigments
BlackDiamondPigments.com, JessCrow.com/resources

MIXING CUPS
big-box store, home improvement store

MIXING STICKS, SILICONE OR WOODEN (CRAFT STICKS OR TONGUE DEPRESSORS)
art store, drugstore, pharmacy, grocery store, JessCrow.com/resources

MOLDS (SILICONE)
Crafted Elements
CraftedElements.com, JessCrow.com/resources

PIGMENTS, DISPERSION
TotalBoat
TotalBoat.com

PIGMENTS, LIQUID
MIXOL 12-Piece Kit
Mixol.com, JessCrow.com/resources

PLASTIC SHEETING (UHMW OR HDPE)
specialty plastic store, JessCrow.com/resources

SANDPAPER
Woodcraft, big-box store, home improvement store

SPRAY-PAINT BOOTH (COLLAPSIBLE)
Wagner Spraytech Spray Shelter
Home improvement store, JessCrow.com/resources

TAPE, PAINTER'S AND TUCK
Woodcraft, big-box store, home improvement store

TOTES, RUBBER OR PLASTIC
big-box store, home improvement store

TOOLS

ANGLE GRINDER
DeWalt Angle Grinder Tool Kit with Bag and Cutting
    Wheels (DW840K)
big-box store, home improvement store, JessCrow
    .com/resources

BRUSHES
Artlicious Paint Brush Set (25-Pack)
art store, big-box store, home improvement store,
    JessCrow.com/resources

CA GLUE
Starbond Multi-Purpose Medium High-Performance
    Premium Cyanoacrylate Instant Adhesive
Home improvement store, JessCrow.com/resources

CHIP BRUSH
Pro Grade 24-Piece Variety Set
big-box store, home improvement store, JessCrow
    .com/resources

DEBURRING TOOL
AFA Tooling Deburring Tool
Home improvement store, JessCrow.com/resources

DRILL
Festool drill
Woodcraft, home improvement store, JessCrow.com/
    resources

HEAT GUN
Wagner FURNO 300
(Pay attention to the trigger on this model. The cor-
    rect 300 has a red lever, not a black rocker.)
Wagner-Group.com, big-box store, home improve-
    ment store, JessCrow.com/resources

HEATING PAD
drugstore, pharmacy, big-box store, home improve-
    ment store

LEVEL
big-box store, home improvement store, JessCrow
    .com/resources

PLIERS
Husky 4-Piece Pliers Set
big-box store, home improvement store, JessCrow
    .com/resources

ROTARY GRINDER (DREMEL)
Dremel 4000
big-box store, home improvement store, JessCrow
    .com/resources

SANDER
DeWalt Random Orbit Sander (5-inch) or Festool
Woodcraft, big-box store, home improvement store,
    JessCrow.com/resources

SCALE (KITCHEN)
grocery store, big-box store, home improvement
    store, JessCrow.com/resources
Thermometer (room)
drugstore, pharmacy, grocery store, big-box store,
    home improvement store, JessCrow.com/
    resources

TIMER
grocery store, big-box store, home improvement
    store, JessCrow.com/resources

TORCH
big-box store, home improvement store, JessCrow
    .com/resources

UV LIGHT BAR
beauty supply store, big-box store, JessCrow.com/
    resources

PROJECT-SPECIFIC ITEMS

You can find laser and CNC files for the projects in this book at JessCrow.com/book-cut-files

Bookmark

6-Pack DIY Bookmark Resin Mold Rectangle Bookmark Silicone Molds
JessCrow.com/book-projects

Coasters

Wooden Coasters for Drinks, Set of 4
JessCrow.com/book-projects

Wave Wall Art

Surfboard
Surfboard-Shaped Serving and Cutting Board
Liquid pigment in white
JessCrow.com/book-projects

Wall Clock

Wooden Clock Round: Walnut Hollow 27636 Baltic Birch Gallery Clock Surface (14-inch diameter x 0.35-inch)
Alcohol Ink Set
Glitter-style mica powder: "Starry Night" Black Diamond Pigment
Round Router Jig: Milescraft 1219 Circle Guide Kit (Cutter Jig)
UV resin and curing light: TotalBoat 200g UV Cure Clear Acrylic Resin with UV Flashlight
JessCrow.com/book-projects

Kitchen Knife

Blank Knife
Holographic Paint: FolkArt Dragonfly Glaze Multi-Surface Paint, Full Spectrum
Holographic Shrink-Wrap Film
Knife Blank: Sarge Knives Custom Folding Knife Kits
Silicone Knife Scale Mold: WoodRiver Silicone Knife Scale Mold (Dual Cavity)
JessCrow.com/book-projects

Lazy Suzan

10-inch Acacia Wood Lazy Susan Organizers
Lazy Susan hardware: 6-inch Lazy Susan Turntable (Steel Ball Bearing Rotating Tray)
JessCrow.com/book-projects

End Table

Wooden End Table: Side Table Round (natural walnut)
Ghost Gold Mica Powder: Black Diamond Pigments Mica Powder Variety Pack 9 (10 Ghost Colors)
JessCrow.com/book-projects

River Dining Table

Wooden slab table
Festool 574432 Domino Joiner DF 500 Q Set
JessCrow.com/book-projects

Chaos Table

36-inch diameter Wood Tabletop
Painter's Putty '53': DAP Painter's Putty '53'
Putty Knife: Flex Nylon Handle Putty Knife
Black Pipe Table Leg Kit
JessCrow.com/book-projects

INDEX